TENNESSEE TALES
THE TEXTBOOKS DON'T TELL

Jennie Ivey
W. Calvin Dickinson
Lisa W. Rand

The Overmountain Press

JOHNSON CITY, TENNESSEE

Front-Cover Drawing by Michael Birdwell
Back-Cover Photo by Richard Rand

Edited by Jason Weems
Book Design by Cherisse McGinty
Jacket Design by Stacey Amos

Hardcover ISBN 1-57072-244-7
Trade Paper ISBN 1-57072-235-8

4 5 6 7 8 9 0

To my many friends whose encouragement and enthusiasm kept me writing, and especially to my family, who often "made do without the mama" during the months I was working on this book.

J. I.

To the students in my History of Tennessee classes who made teaching the course so interesting.

W. C. D.

To my little girl, Victoria, whose excitement about the characters in this book have kept me excited about Tennessee history, and to my husband, Richard, for his constant support and encouragement.

L. W. R.

ACKNOWLEDGMENTS

The Authors would like to thank the following people:

Amber Barfield, Metro Archives
Joanne Barthel, Standard Candy Company
Colin Baxter, ETSU
Michael Birdwell, TTU
Tracy Boyd, Tennessee Walking Horse Breeders' and Exhibitors' Assocation (TWHBEA)
Bob Cherry, TWHBEA
Charles Cooper
Judy Duke, Cookeville History Museum
Elizabeth Ehrensing, The Coca-Cola Company
Ken Fieth, Metro Archives of Nashville and Davidson County
Edwin G. Frank, Curator of Special Collections and
       Associate Professor of Libraries, The University of Memphis
Peggy Gillespie
Sara Gillespie
Bob Good, Mailboxes, Etc.
Susan Gordon, Tennessee State Library Association (TSLA)
Joe Groom
Jack Gunter, photographer
Jere Hargrove, Tennessee State Representative
Annette Hartigan, Great Smoky Mountains National Park Library (GSMNPL)
Steven Hayes, Tennessee Department of Corrections Public Information Officer
Kelly Hill, Graceland
Karl and Susie Klein, photographers
Catherine Ann McConnaughay, Oak Ridge Public Library (ORPL)
Betty McDowell
Larry Medley
Morgan County Library staff
Sally Polhemus, McClung Collection
Bets Ramsey
Dick Rand
Susan Sherwood, Graceland
Joan Tansil
Brenda Turnage
Judy Underwood, *Morgan County News*
Merikay Waldvogel
James Edward Wescott, photographer
Debbie Williams, Brushy Mountain Correctional Complex
Tracy Lauritzen Wright, registrar, National Civil Rights Museum, Memphis
Andy York

INTRODUCTION

As I sat as a student in Calvin Dickinson's Tennessee History course not long ago and listened to him regale the class with one fascinating story after another, I made an important discovery.

History the way he was teaching it was not only painless, it was fun. It was nothing more nor less than the stories of men and women whose actions and ideas helped shape our state into what it was and what it is—people who were really no different than people are today, however much the times we live in seem to have changed.

I had taught history myself several years earlier, but much of that material was new to me. "Did that really happen?" I'd ask him after hearing a particularly outlandish tale. "I sure never knew that," I'd find myself muttering over and over again. And finally, "Somebody ought to write these stories down."

Thus was born the idea for this book.

Then we discovered Lisa Rand, whose expertise in and love for children's literature seemed to make her a natural partner in our endeavor to make history not only enlightening but also entertaining for young readers.

We wrote *Tennessee Tales* with seventh graders in mind because they are the ones who study Tennessee history as part of their curriculum, but we hope that readers of all ages will enjoy the stories.

This book is not intended to be a comprehensive text. It is simply a collection of snippets from the past of what surely must be the most fascinating of all the fifty of our United States.

All the stories contained herein are true and are as historically accurate as it was possible to make them. In some cases, realistic dialogue was created in order to enliven the action. If it seems, in the telling of these stories, that a little extra jam has been added to the biscuit, perhaps it has—not to distort the taste but simply to make it all the more enjoyable going down.

—Jennie Ivey

TABLE OF CONTENTS

THE LITTLEST CHEROKEE WARRIOR

How Dragging Canoe Earned His Name

"No. You can't go."

The Indian boy had heard those words many times. Whenever he begged to go with the men of the village to hunt or to fight other tribes, his father's answer was always the same.

"You're too young!"

The boy looked up into his father's dark brown eyes. "Please, Father, let me go. I'm not a baby anymore. I'll soon be a man." He stretched his arms out from his sides and curled his hands toward his shoulders. "Look how big my muscles have grown!"

The man smiled. "Yes, son, every day you are growing older and bigger and stronger, but you are not ready to be a warrior. That time will come soon enough."

The boy sighed, but he said nothing more. His father was Attakullakulla, one of the most important chiefs of the Cherokee people. He was well respected by his own people and by other Indian tribes. White men respected him, too. When Attakullakulla was a young man, he and six other Cherokees had visited King George II in London.

But even if Attakullakulla had not been a chief, the boy would not have argued with him. Cherokee children did not disagree with their elders.

"Go now and find your mother," Attakullakulla said. "I'm sure she can find plenty of work for a boy with such big muscles."

His father was right. It would soon be harvest time. The boy's

Attakullakulla in London, 1730
(Sketch by artist Hogarth, courtesy TSLA)

mother and the other women would need help gathering the corn, beans, and squash and storing them for the winter ahead.

Before long, the Cherokee people would move out of their big, airy summer houses and into the tiny, round log huts where they lived when the weather turned cold.

The boy hated wintertime. When ice and snow lay thick on the ground and the wind howled through the trees, the women and children had to stay indoors for many days at a time. A low fire burned all day and night inside the hut, but there were no windows or chimney. It was cramped and dark and so smoky that it made the boy's eyes burn and his chest hurt. There was nothing to do but stare at the fire and hope that spring would come soon.

The boy longed to be a grown man. In winter, the men didn't have to stay inside. They took long hunting trips and were often gone from the village for several days at a time.

When they returned, they would bring the wild game they had killed—elk, deer, bear, and turkey. Then there would be a grand celebration. Some of the meat would be roasted and eaten right away. The rest would be cut into strips and dried into jerky that would not spoil. That's what the people would eat until the men went on another hunt.

It was always more fun when the men were home. They showed the boys how to make bows and arrow shafts from hickory wood. They taught them to wrestle and made them swim in icy waters so they would learn to be tough.

The men coached the boys in lacrosse, a game played with sticks that had nets on one end. Players used their sticks to throw, catch, and carry a ball—a deerskin pouch stuffed with moss or hair—toward their team's goal. They also used the sticks as clubs and sometimes hurt each other. Cherokee men and boys thought lacrosse was fun, but it was also good practice for battle.

Of course, Cherokee boys weren't allowed to take part in real battles. When the grown men went to fight against other tribes, they left the boys at home with the women and little children.

In 1752 Attakullakulla's son was twelve years old. He was not as tall as a man and his shoulders were not as broad, but he could shinny up a sycamore tree quicker than anyone in the village. No one could run a footrace faster. He could shoot an arrow clear across the widest meadow. He could catch a speckled trout with his bare hands. With one puff upon a blowgun, he could kill a fat quail.

The boy was ready to be a Cherokee warrior, even if his father didn't think so.

The men of his village were preparing to go to war against the Shawnee Indians. The Shawnees had been hunting on lands claimed by the Cherokees and had killed some Cherokee people, so the men of his tribe were going to seek revenge. More than anything in the world, the boy wanted to go along. But he knew what his father would say if he asked.

"No. You're too young!"

This time, he wouldn't ask.

The night before the war party was to leave, the boy lay awake in the darkness of the hut until his family was asleep. Silently, he pulled on his buckskin shirt and leggings. He tied his moccasins tightly onto his feet. There was an early autumn chill in the air, so he took the bearskin blanket from his bunk and wrapped it around his shoulders.

Then he slipped into the forest.

For many years the boy had practiced walking in the woods without making a sound. He knew he must be careful not to crunch leaves or break sticks as he walked because the noise would scare animals away. A cough or a sneeze could mean death if an enemy warrior was near.

But tonight the boy was not worried about animals or enemy warriors. He was thinking only about Attakullakulla, who would send him back to the women if he discovered what the boy was doing.

A half-moon shone on the path that led to the river. The boy walked for a long time. He had never been this far from the village by himself. His legs were growing tired. He hoped he had not taken the wrong trail.

When he heard the sound of running water, he smiled. Through the darkness he could see dozens of dugout canoes lined up along the riverbank. The boats had been pulled far up onto the bank and turned upside down so that the water wouldn't wash them away.

Some of the canoes were long and very heavy. They had been carved from the tallest trees in the forest. It would take several men to paddle one of those big boats. Other canoes were shorter and much lighter in weight. The boy searched until he found the smallest canoe. He squeezed under it, curled into a tight ball, and pulled the bearskin blanket up to his chin.

Then he fell asleep.

The sound of his father's voice awakened him. The boy opened his eyes and peeked out from his hiding place. The sky had turned pink. The sun would be up soon. Attakullakulla was talking to his men, telling them which canoes to turn over and put into the river.

The boy lay very still. He hoped none of the warriors would come near his hiding place. After the men had paddled down the river, the boy thought he could follow them in the small canoe. By the time they discovered him, it might be too late to send him home.

But things didn't work out that way.

"You two," Attakullakulla said, pointing to the youngest warriors in the group, "take that small canoe over there."

The warriors walked over to where the boy was hiding. With trembling fingers, the boy pulled the bearskin clear over his head. His heart was beating so hard it seemed to shake the ground. He held his breath and lay still as a stone. Maybe the warriors wouldn't notice him.

Standing at either end of the boat, the young men lifted it and flipped it over.

"What's this doing here?" they said with surprise when they saw the bearskin. One of the warriors reached down and picked it up. Then both young men began to laugh. They laughed so hard that their sides shook and tears ran down their cheeks. When the other warriors heard them, they wanted to know what was so funny.

Attakullakulla wanted to know what was so funny, too. He walked over to see what was going on.

The boy began to tremble. What would his father do? Would he make him stay here, alone? Would he send him back to the village? Would he punish him some other way?

The chief did not laugh. He did not even smile. But he didn't seem angry, either.

Words began to tumble out of the boy's mouth. "Please, Father, please. Let me go this time. You said yourself that I am almost a man. I will keep up with the other warriors. I will fight bravely. I will—"

Attakullakulla gently pressed two fingers over the boy's lips. "Do not talk, my son. Listen. I do not think you are old enough to travel with us yet, but I will make this offer. If you can carry your own canoe, all by yourself, then you may come along. The other men cannot help you—they have their own boats to take care of."

"But Father, why will I need to *carry* my canoe? Canoes are for paddling, and I am good at that!"

"You will see, son. You will see."

Attakullakulla turned and walked away. The boy grinned. He did not have to go back to the women and be treated like a child. He would show his father that he was right to take him along.

"I will paddle harder and faster than anyone in the group," the boy whispered to himself. "I will lead the warriors up the river and I will fight bravely. My father will not be sorry I am with him. He will be proud that I am here!"

The boy stood behind his canoe, just as the other warriors did. When Attakullakulla gave the signal, he bent and shoved it toward the river. As the boat slipped into the water, he leaped aboard and took up his paddle. He lifted his face to the sky.

"Today I am a man!" he shouted.

All morning the boy paddled up the river alongside the other warriors. The sun shone on his bare chest and shoulders. Soon it became very warm. The boy's arms grew tired, but he didn't complain.

When the sun was high up in the sky, his father gave the order for the men to pull their boats ashore. "We will rest here for a while," Attakullakulla said. "Then we will carry our canoes across land until we are past the rapids."

The chief looked at his son. Neither of them said a word. The boy felt a lump growing in his throat. The time had come to prove that he was indeed a man.

The boy ate some of the jerky he had brought with him. He went to the river and filled his cupped hands with cool water, but he did not really drink. He watched as the warriors heaved the boats onto their strong shoulders and began walking into the woods.

Would he be able to do that, too?

When everyone was gone, the boy walked over to his canoe. He squatted down and tried to pick it up. He strained until every vein in his neck bulged and rivulets of sweat ran down his sides, but he couldn't even lift the front end. He knew the back end would be no easier, but he tried it anyway. It wouldn't budge.

It had been easy to push the canoe down the bank and into the river and to paddle it on the gentle waters. But it was going to be impossible to carry it—the canoe was just too heavy.

Attakullakulla and the other men were already out of sight. The sound of their voices grew more and more faint. If the boy couldn't keep up, his father might leave him there, alone. Worse yet, he might send him back to the women. The boy could not bear to let that happen.

He could not paddle the canoe on land and he could not carry it. But there was one way that he could move it—he could drag it!

And that's exactly what he did.

With all the strength that was in him, the boy began pulling the heavy canoe through the forest. When his right arm grew tired, he pulled with his left arm. When he grew too tired to pull, he pushed. His face was red and his breathing loud and shallow, but the look of determination on his face never changed. He never stopped to rest and he never grew discouraged. He was a Cherokee warrior, and Cherokee warriors didn't give up.

After what seemed like a very long time, the boy heard the sound of gently running water. He was past the rapids at last, and suddenly he was too happy to feel tired. He had moved his own canoe, all by himself. The boy put both hands inside the boat and began pulling it with all his might toward the river.

He did not know that the men had gathered to watch, until they began to shout. *"Tsi·yu gansi·ni. Tsi·yu gansi·ni.* He is dragging the canoe!"

The boy turned and saw his father walking toward him. Attakullakulla was smiling. He put his hands on the boy's shoulders. "My son," he said, "you have proved today that you are tough and brave and strong. From now on, you will no longer be called a boy. You are a man. And you will have a new name—a man's name.

"From this day forward, you will be called Dragging Canoe. And I predict that you will become the greatest of all Cherokee warriors."

Attakullakulla was right. Dragging Canoe (1740-1792) did grow up to become the greatest of all Cherokee warriors. But it was fighting white settlers, not other Indian tribes, which brought him fame.

By the early 1760s, Americans hungry for new land and new adventure began moving from Virginia and North Carolina across the Appalachian Mountains into what would become the states of Tennessee and Kentucky. Some Cherokee leaders, including Attakullakulla, wanted to live in peace with the

Chickamauga Warrior Dragging Canoe
(Sketch by Bernie Andrews)

white settlers. They traded vast quantities of Indian land for little more than trinkets and empty promises.

Dragging Canoe urged his people not to negotiate with the white settlers. "Whole Indian nations have melted away like snowballs in the sun before the white man's advance," he told them. "Soon the whole Indian race will be extinct."

His words were not heeded. Cherokee leaders continued to sign treaties with the white settlers. "You have bought a fair land," Dragging Canoe warned the men who purchased the Indians' sacred hunting grounds. "But there is a cloud hanging over it. You will find its settlement dark and bloody."

Dragging Canoe spent the last years of his life trying to make those words come true. He fought many battles against white settlers. He even started a new tribe—the Chickamaugas—whose mission was to stop white encroachment at any cost. He failed. White settlers continued to pour across the mountains by the thousands.

Several years after Dragging Canoe died, his predictions came true. In 1838, nearly16,000 Cherokees were forced to move to Oklahoma on a journey now known as the Trail of Tears. More than 4,000 of them died on that journey.

The young Indian boy who proved he was man enough to move his own canoe is now considered one of the greatest heroes of the Cherokee people.

BIBLIOGRAPHY

Bruchac, Joseph. *The Trail of Tears*. New York: Random House, 1999.

Museum of the Cherokee Indian, Cherokee, N. C. 1999. <http://www.cherokeemuseum.org> (July 15, 2002).

Satz, Ronald. *Tennessee's Indian Peoples: From White Contact to Removal, 1540-1840*. Knoxville: University of Tennessee Press, 1979.

Smith, D. Ray. "Dragging Canoe, Cherokee War Chief." <http://members.tripod.com/~SmithDRay/draggingcanoe-index-9.html> (July 15, 2002).

Chapter Two

HOW MUCH LONGER TILL WE GET THERE?

Rachel Donelson Floats to Nashville

Rachel Donelson was excited. But she was a little bit frightened, too. She and her family were leaving their home in western Virginia for what Rachel was sure would be a grand new adventure.

Her father, Colonel John Donelson, had been asked to lead a flotilla of boats from Fort Patrick Henry, which lay west across the Appalachian Mountains, to the Big Salt Lick, in the middle of what soon would become the territory of Tennessee.

Colonel Donelson was an important man in Virginia. He had served in several elected offices, including the House of Burgesses. But now he was eager to seek a new life and new fortunes in lands to the west.

"Where will we live after we cross the mountains, Papa?" thirteen-year-old Rachel asked.

"There are cabins in Tennessee at Fort Patrick Henry," he answered. "We'll live in one of them, but only for a little while."

"Till winter is over?"

"No, child, we'll be leaving the fort about the time winter's getting started. Rivers are easier to travel during the cold months because the water's swifter and deeper. We'll only live at Fort Patrick Henry long enough to build the boats."

"What will happen to our furniture, Papa, and our animals?"

"Most of the furniture will have to be sold before we leave Virginia, Rachel. There'll be no room for it in our wagon, and even less room on the boat. I've promised your mama that we'll take the sugar

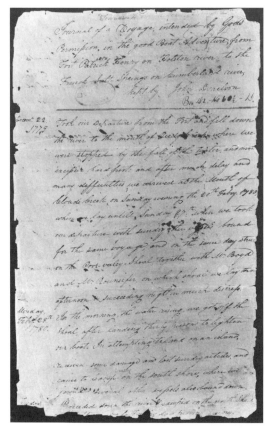

A page from Colonel John Donelson's journal, in which he recorded what happened on the river voyage. (Courtesy TSLA)

chest that belonged to your grandmother, and her sewing rocker if it will fit. Everything else will have to stay here. When we get to the Big Salt Lick, your brothers and I will build more furniture. I promise."

"But can't we take the piano, Papa? I'm just getting good at playing 'Greensleeves.' You can't build a piano. Papa, please...."

"I wish we could, Rachel, but it's just too big and heavy. The road through the mountains is littered with pianos folks have thrown off their wagons. Better to sell it for cash than to burn it for firewood."

"What about the dogs? And the pigs? And the chickens? And—"

John Donelson laughed. "They won't be left behind, that I can promise you. The dogs will travel on the boats with us. They can hear and smell an Indian long before we can. And we'll take the chickens, too. I doubt they'll be laying many eggs in this weather, but they'll make mighty tasty stew if rabbits and squirrels are scarce. Captain Robertson's men will drive the cattle and horses with them."

Captain James Robertson had been chosen to lead a group of men overland from Fort Patrick Henry to the Big Salt Lick, through the Cumberland Gap and along the Wilderness Road. Their wives and children would make the river journey with Colonel Donelson and forty other men. Although the route by water was longer, it was considered much safer.

"What will happen to our pigs, Papa?"

Rachel Donelson was a farm girl, and she knew that pigs were the most important of all farm animals. They were smart and easy to train, they would eat anything, and a single boar and sow could produce dozens of offspring in a very short time.

But the best thing about pigs was that every part of them was useful for something. Rachel's mama liked to say you could use every part of the pig but the squeal. Ham, bacon, sausage, and fresh side meat for the table. Chitterlings as a special treat for the slaves. Lard for soap and candles, and for seasoning greens. Hair for stuffing mattresses. Even the pigs' bladders were used, filled with air to make kickballs for children's play.

"We'll carry pork in our saddlebags," Colonel Donelson said, "cut up and salted and ready to eat if we can't find enough fresh meat on our hunts. Robertson's men will take some live pigs on the trail to the Big Salt Lick."

Rachel tossed her dark curls and flashed a smile at her father. "I can hardly wait to get started."

The weeks at Fort Patrick Henry flew by. The women stayed busy preparing meals and knitting scarves and stockings for the cold months ahead.

The men spent long hours cutting logs and assembling the flatboats and covered dugout canoes known as *pirogues*. After the boats were built, the men loaded cured meats, barrels of molasses, sacks of cornmeal and flour and salt, and bundles of clothing and bedcovers onto them.

The Donelsons' flatboat was named the *Adventure*. It was twenty feet wide and 100 feet long, constructed of heavy, squared timbers. The sides were built six feet high for protection from Indian gunfire. The roof that covered most of the boat created a cabin for cooking and sleeping.

On December 22, with the *Adventure* leading the way, Colonel Donelson gave the order to depart. The boats floated only three miles before they became icebound.

Rachel was bored. And cold. And though she wouldn't admit it even to herself, she was afraid. She and the others traveling with

The *Adventure* was similar to the flatboat in this sketch. (Courtesy TSLA)

her did not know that the winter of 1779-80 would be known as "The Cold Winter" for many years afterwards.

They did not know that the Holston River would become a solid sheet of ice, so thick that the strongest man with the sharpest ax could not break it.

They did not know that the band of Cherokee Indians known as Chickamaugas had returned to villages along the riverbanks and were watching the white settlers' every move.

They did not know that thirty-three of the nearly 200 persons who began the journey would die before it was over.

They did not know that they were taking part in one of the most famous river voyages in American history.

But they did know that food supplies were low, and that if the journey did not recommence soon, they might all starve before reaching the Big Salt Lick. Sacks of flour and cornmeal, full and plentiful when the trip began, were dwindling quickly. Most of the preserved meat had already been eaten.

"Why can't the boys shoot us a deer or a bear, Papa?" Rachel asked.

"I wish they could, Rachel, but it's not that easy. Bears are hibernating this time of year—you know that. It would be blind luck for your brothers to happen upon a den. And the deer have moved deep into the woods trying to find food. This weather is as hard on animals as it is on us."

Worry showed in John Donelson's kind eyes. Rachel thought how lucky she was to have him for her father. He was brave and still physically strong at the age of sixty, and he knew how to survive in the wilderness. Years of working as a surveyor had made him familiar with the land. And he had dealt with Indians, in both peace and war, for many years.

Rachel knew that no matter what hardships they faced, John Donelson would take care of his family and the rest of the people in the flotilla.

Huddled next to the hearth, Rachel looked around the cabin of the *Adventure*. The room that had once seemed so cozy and charming was now closing in on her. How much longer could thirty people call this tiny place home without going crazy?

The firebox had no chimney—only a small hole cut in the roof that seemed to draw in great quantities of frigid air but which let out very little smoke. The cabin was dark except for the glow of the fire and the few candles placed about so that the people inside could go about their daily chores.

There was no real furniture. The cabin was just wall-to-wall beds, crude bunks suspended from the walls, and pallets laid end-to-end on the floor.

Worst of all was the smell. Baths under those conditions were impossible, and since there was no way to wash dirty clothes, most folks had given up the notion of changing into clean ones.

The heavy scent of grease and turnip greens and burnt bacon permeated the walls and ceiling and floor.

And the chickens! Rachel was sure that she would never grow accustomed to the smell of chickens. Back home in Virginia, the rooster and hens had roamed freely, scratching for bugs at the back steps and roosting at night in the low trees in the yard. They had never been allowed inside.

The only smell Rachel had ever associated with chickens was the delightful aroma that filled the house when the cook fried them for Sunday dinner. But the chicken aroma that filled the cabin was anything but delightful. Even Rachel's mother, who almost never complained, found it hard to be silent.

"Not an egg since we left Virginia," she muttered. "Seems to me the best thing to do is go ahead and cook them all, before they get too old and tough to chew."

And it wasn't long before that happened, since the men often returned from their hunts with nothing to show but frostbitten fingers and empty tow sacks.

Rachel Donelson was the oldest of her parents' "second family." She had four brothers and three sisters that were already grown adults, and all of them were making the journey to the Big Salt Lick. Brother William was traveling overland with James Robertson's men. The rest of the family was on the Donelson boat.

Her brother Johnny had even brought his sixteen-year-old bride, Mary Purnell Donelson, along. Young Mary had looked forward to the voyage as her honeymoon trip!

Rachel's three younger brothers were her constant companions and playmates. So were Captain Robertson's five children, who were traveling with their mother on the *Adventure*.

It was too cold and dangerous for the children to play outside on the snow-covered riverbanks. Chilblains were a near certainty and Indian warriors a constant worry. The children tried to amuse themselves indoors with word puzzles and guessing games, with checkers and marbles and jacks. Rachel even made up her mind to teach her six-year-old brother, Leven, to read, but he was a reluctant student.

For farm children accustomed to spending most of their daylight hours outdoors, time inside the cramped little cabin seemed to crawl.

"How much longer till we go?" the children whined. "How many more days?"

Colonel Donelson never lost patience, but his answer was always the same. "When the good Lord sees fit to send a thaw, we'll leave. Until then, we'll have to be content just to watch and wait."

And wait they did. They could not go forward and they could not go back. It was not until February 27, sixty-eight days after they had departed Fort Patrick Henry, that the ice on the river finally melted. As Colonel Donelson's order to "Shove Off!" was repeated down the line of boats, Rachel thought they were the sweetest words she'd ever heard.

They had floated only a few hours, when the *Adventure* became hung on sharp rocks jutting out of the river. No matter how hard the men shoved with their long steering poles, the boat wouldn't come loose.

"You boys are going to have to get in the water," Rachel's father told her older brothers. "Lash those ropes to the stern and see if you can pull us off the rocks."

Rachel shivered at the thought of the icy waters, but she knew that her brothers would not refuse. While they pulled and tugged at the ropes, those left on board shoved the poles against the rocks with all their might. But it was no use. The boat would not budge.

"It's just too heavy," her father said. "We've got to do something to lighten the load."

Rachel looked around at the contents of the boat. What could be thrown off? To survive the trip, they needed everything that was on board. How could they make the boat lighter?

She looked at her brothers in the chest-deep river. Their lips were blue and their teeth were chattering.

"Papa, I'll get out," Rachel said softly. "That will help some."

"I'm afraid you're right, Rachel. Most of us are going to have to get in the water, or we're never going to get the boat loose."

The people on board quickly began shedding their bulky outer garments. Only old Callie the cook and Mrs. Robertson's babies were to stay on the boat. Rachel took a deep breath, closed her eyes, and plunged into the icy water. She thought at first that she had never felt anything so cold in her life, but within seconds her body became so numb that she could no longer feel anything.

"Everybody shove with all your might," her father was shouting. "If we don't get this boat free and us out of this water soon, we shall all surely perish!"

They pushed with every ounce of muscle and will that was in them. Finally, the *Adventure* slid off the rocks. Holding tightly to the towropes, Rachel's brothers pulled the huge boat to the bank of a nearby island. They built campfires and huddled around them, thawing frozen hands and feet and turning, turning, turning until their clothes and skin steamed and finally dried.

Rachel laid her head on her arms, curled herself toward the fire, and slept until morning.

Less than a week later, the flotilla passed the mouth of the French Broad River, near the site where the town of Knoxville would be built. They were on the Tennessee River now, and that made Rachel happy. At long last they were moving on, floating through the great valleys of East Tennessee, in fog so thick she could almost taste it on her tongue.

She didn't even need to ask Papa how much longer it would be till they got to the Big Salt Lick. It was bound to be any day now.

One of the smaller boats capsized on the second day of March. When the others stopped to help, a boy named Reuben Harrison decided to go ashore to hunt. No one tried to dissuade him. The supply of cured meat was completely gone and there was not a chicken, tough and stringy or otherwise, left on any of the boats. Maybe he would happen upon a deer or a flock of wild turkeys.

But when darkness fell, there was no sign of Reuben. The men fired their guns. No shot answered. Mrs. Harrison was crazy with grief. Her cries of "My boy is lost! He's lost forever!" echoed through the night. No one slept.

Colonel Donelson sent search parties into the woods as soon as the sun was up the next morning, but Reuben was nowhere to be found. They left Mr. Harrison and some others to continue the search. The *Adventure* and most of the other boats went on.

About midmorning, one of the men spotted a figure far up the shore, waving his arms and shouting. It was Reuben—cold, tired, and frightened nearly to death. His mother rushed to him and threw her arms around him and didn't seem to care one bit that he hadn't killed a deer, or even a rabbit.

But Rachel did. If Reuben was going to be gone so long and cause so much worry, the least he could have done was bring them back something for the stewpot.

The flotilla passed the mouth of the Clinch River the next day and was joined by several boats from a nearby fort. That night, one of the slaves died. He had been suffering from gangrene—an infection that can be caused by frozen feet and legs. His death was to be the first of many that the river travelers would suffer over the next few weeks.

It had been raining hard for days. When the rains finally stopped, the stiff March winds began to blow, kicking up waves that slapped high on the sides of the *Adventure*'s cabin. Colonel Donelson issued the order for all boats to pull ashore. Though the

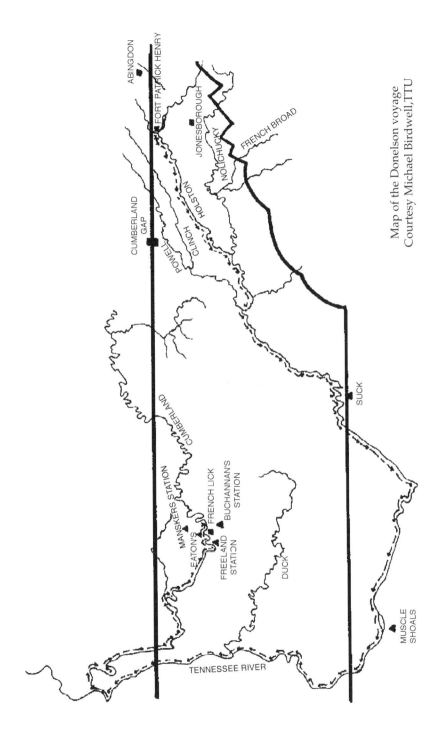

Map of the Donelson voyage
Courtesy Michael Birdwell, TTU

flatboats could have gone on despite the rough current, the pirogues could not.

"What is this place, Papa?" Rachel asked as she clambered onto dry land. "It looks like somebody used to live here."

"That they did, Rachel. The Indian leader named Dragging Canoe had a town that stood at this very spot."

Rachel looked around. This was land that had been farmed not long ago. Dried cornstalks waved in the wind, and rotting squash and pumpkins littered the ground. Charred remains of burned-out cabins stood at the outskirts of the field.

"Did the Indians burn their own village, Papa?" Rachel's dark eyes were wide with fear.

"No, Rachel. Colonel Shelby's men burned several Chickamauga villages last spring because the Indians had been attacking white settlers."

"Where are Dragging Canoe's people now?"

"That, my dear, is something we can't know for sure. I suspect they're not too very far from here."

Chickamauga warriors created no fear for the children that day, however. It was the first time in more than two months that they had been able to run and jump and holler and play to their hearts' content. Though the sky was gray and the wind sharp, the bitter bite of winter was gone. The children frolicked among the buttercups and newly green violets until dark.

And on that day, in the midst of the burned-out Indian village, the settlers' number increased by one. Mrs. Ephriam Peyton, whose husband was traveling overland with Captain Robertson, gave birth to a baby boy.

It seemed that fortune was finally smiling down on the weary voyagers.

The good times did not last long. The flotilla cast off late the next morning, moving swiftly in the rain-swollen current.

Rachel heard the Indians before she saw them. "Brothers, how do ye do? Come ashore," they were saying.

Squinting ahead, she could see a large number of Indians lining the riverbank, smiling and waving. "Papa, they look friendly," she said with surprise.

"Father, let me take a canoe and go ashore to meet them," Johnny said. "Perhaps Colonel Shelby's men have taught them a lesson and they are ready to seek peace."

But before Johnny's small boat could reach the bank, half a dozen Indian canoes approached the *Adventure*. Several young warriors sprang aboard.

"I am Archie Coody," one of them said.

Rachel huddled in a front corner of the boat's cabin, peering at the stranger through a crack between the logs. She had never before been so close to a real Indian, and her heart beat fast with excitement.

Her younger brother Sam, wedged in next to her, spoke in an excited whisper. "That man has blue eyes, Rachel, and his skin is not brown like the others. Do you suppose he's really an Indian?"

"I'm not sure," Rachel replied. "Perhaps his father was a long hunter who married an Indian woman."

"Do you think they'll hurt us?"

"Papa doesn't seem to think so. He's smiling and handing out ribbons and tobacco. Be still and let's see if we can hear what they're saying."

"Your young men must not cross the river," Archie Coody said. "Call them back and move quickly to put the Indian villages behind you. Then all you will have to worry about is the fearsome Suck." He smiled and shook hands with Colonel Donelson. Then he and his companions departed.

Rachel and Sam looked at each other and grinned. The river might be frightening, but at least they didn't have to worry about Indians anymore.

They were wrong. Within minutes after the Chickamaugas left the *Adventure*, one of the settlers lay dead. The Indians had shot him when his boat ventured too close to the riverbank. But that was not the worst of it.

Early in the journey, smallpox had spread among the twenty-eight people who were traveling on Thomas Stuart's boat. Colonel Donelson knew allowing that boat to travel close to the others would expose everyone on the journey to the deadly disease, so he had ordered Stuart to travel far back, at the end of the flotilla.

The other boats were well ahead of the quarantined vessel when the Indians surrounded it.

Rachel would never forget the horrible sounds she heard when the Indians captured the Stuart boat. Gunshots rang out, followed by Indian war whoops and screams of "No! Please, no! Help us, please!"

"Father," Johnny yelled over the roar of the river. "We've got to go back and try to save them."

"There's no way, son. No way. The current's just too strong. And it's too late to help them anyway. They are doomed. May God rest their souls. And may the curse of the smallpox be visited a thousand times over upon the Indians."

Colonel Donelson's voice caught in his throat, and for the first time ever in her thirteen years, Rachel saw a tear trickle down her father's cheek.

Only minutes after tragedy befell the Stuart boat, the river suddenly became very narrow and deep. The Cumberland Mountains jutted sharply into the tight passageway, so close it seemed that Rachel could almost reach out and touch the rocky faces of the mountains.

"Is this the Suck, Father?" she asked.

"Yes it is, child. See how the water gurgles and swirls? That's why the Indians call it the Boiling Pot. We'll have to be careful not to let the boats smash into the rocks. The flatboats shouldn't have much trouble, but I worry that the pirogues will be tossed about."

But it was not the fierce water that was to cause the most trouble.

Looking up, the travelers could see hundreds of Indian warriors lining the high bluffs above them. On signal, they lifted their rifles and began to fire. But the river was carrying the flotilla along so swiftly, and the Indians were firing from such a distance, that no one was killed. Four people were wounded, but only slightly.

Almost as suddenly as it had narrowed, the river widened again. The current became gentle, and Colonel Donelson began counting the members of his fleet.

"Are they all here, John?" Mrs. Donelson asked.

He shook his head slowly, and his face wore the same expression it had when the Stuart boat was captured. "No, my dear, they're not. Jonathan Jennings's boat is missing."

"You don't suppose. . . ."

"Maybe they just fell behind and will catch up in a little while. But if they're too far back, I hate to think what will happen to them."

Rachel wasn't sure exactly what that meant. But she was sure it didn't bode well for the people on Mr. Jennings's boat.

Fearing that the Indians might attack after dark, the flotilla did not tie up to shore that night. They continued to float gently down-river. On the second night, they camped on the north shore, posting watchmen and trusting the dogs to alert them of danger.

It was not yet dawn when the camp was awakened by desperate cries. "Help poor Jennings!" the voice said. "Help poor Jennings!"

Colonel Donelson scrambled from his bunk. "This way, man. This way," he shouted, waving his arms. Mr. Jennings stumbled into camp. He was in wretched condition, his clothes wet and pierced with bullet holes, and his face was covered with cuts and bruises. Behind him were Mrs. Jennings, Mrs. Peyton, and a slave woman.

"Mrs. Peyton, where is your baby?" Rachel asked. "He was on the boat with you, wasn't he?"

Mrs. Peyton turned to Rachel, her eyes filled with a sadness deeper than any Rachel had ever seen. She did not speak.

Mrs. Jennings put her arm around Mrs. Peyton's shoulder. "The baby is gone," she said.

"Gone?" said Rachel. "What do you mean?"

Mr. Jennings spoke. "Our boat was grounded on a rocky shelf and wouldn't move. When the Indians discovered the mess we were in, they opened fire. We began throwing things into the water so that we might lighten the load, but still the boat wouldn't come loose. My son and two other boys panicked and jumped into the water. They were taken prisoner by the Indians."

"No!" Colonel Donelson shouted. "No! How many more souls must we lose before this journey is at an end?"

Jennings continued. "My wife and Mrs. Peyton got into the water to push us off the rocks while I continued to fire at the Indi-ans. By the hand of Providence, the women managed to get the boat loose. We floated quickly with such little weight. The light of your campfires brought us here."

"And the baby?" Rachel asked softly. "Was he taken prisoner, too?"

"No, Rachel. No." Mrs. Jennings said. "The baby was bundled in some of the blankets that were thrown overboard. We didn't discover he was missing until we were nearly at your camp."

Rachel dropped her face into her hands and wept.

They came in sight of Muscle Shoals about ten o'clock the next morning. Rachel's father and Captain Robertson had made an agreement before they left Fort Patrick Henry. If Robertson could find a safe overland passage from the Big Salt Lick to Muscle Shoals, he would leave a sign. The river travelers would abandon their boats and travel north on foot, which would shorten their journey by several hundred miles.

When there was no sign from Captain Robertson—not a blazed tree, nor a letter stuck on a sharp stick—Colonel Donelson assembled his men.

"We can't risk an overland trip when there is no sign from Captain Robertson. We must go on by water, even though it means navigating Muscle Shoals. Get some rest, my friends. It's going to take every bit of strength we've got to make it through what lies ahead."

Rachel had never seen, or even imagined, anything like the shoals. The current ran quickly in every direction. Piles of driftwood were heaped high upon the points of the islands.

"Papa, how long will it take to move through this?"

"That I don't know, dear girl. The water is high. Perhaps the trip will only take a short while."

But Rachel had heard him talking quietly to her mother a few minutes earlier. "The shoals are worse than I ever imagined," he had said. "I fear that our boats will be dashed to pieces, and all our troubles ended at once."

Rachel's first thought was to fall upon her bunk and pull the covers over her head and wait for the end to come. But she was not that kind of girl.

She walked to the open deck and grabbed onto the side of the boat. The wind was blowing hard and the river roared so loudly that the people on board could not even hear each other talk. Rachel had never been to the ocean, but she was sure it could not be louder than this, even during the worst storm.

Her father and brothers gripped their steering poles, knuckles white, ready to push the boat off if it should come too close to the rocks.

For three hours they worked and for three hours Rachel stood and watched them. Every time the boat dragged the bottom of the river, her eyes widened and her heart caught in her throat. Once, the current was so strong that it spun the *Adventure* around in a complete circle, sending all the goods on board crashing into the walls.

But the boat never hung up on the rocks, and they were not dashed to pieces.

By nightfall all the boats were through the shoals, and the occupants camped on the north shore. The travelers looked at each other with amazement. No one was hurt and none of the boats were wrecked. Before they partook of their supper of watery grits, they gave thanks for having made it safely through another day of danger.

For the next week the journey continued with little excitement. Sometimes Indians fired at them from the shore, but they did no real harm. Their biggest enemy now was hunger and fatigue.

Mrs. Donelson's brow, once smooth and unfurrowed, was knit in an almost constant frown. "I don't know how the men can keep on with no food in their stomachs," she said one morning to Rachel. "We have but a few days' supply of cornmeal left and no meat at all."

They had come to the junction of the Tennessee and Ohio rivers, where they would have to travel against the current to reach the Cumberland River. It was here that some of the travelers decided to go their separate ways.

Some chose to float the Ohio downstream to the Mississippi River, where they would head for Natchez. Others were bound north to the Illinois Territory. One of Rachel's sisters and her husband were among this group. As Rachel hugged her sister goodbye, neither of them could stop the tears.

"Will we ever see each other again?" Rachel asked.

"God willing, I believe we will." She kissed Rachel, then turned and departed.

For a month the travelers worked their way upstream, first on the Ohio and then on the Cumberland River.

Sometimes, when the current was so swift that poling the boats did nothing more than keep them in place, the men got into the water and pushed the boats forward. In places where the river was narrow, they lashed ropes to the boats and walked along the shoreline, pulling them.

Colonel Donelson even fashioned a sail from bed sheets and used it to move the *Adventure* along when the wind was blowing. It was slow going, and Rachel was not the only one to wonder if they would ever reach the Big Salt Lick.

"I'm hungry, Mama," her little brothers complained. "I wish we'd stayed in Virginia. How much longer till we get there?"

Mrs. Donelson patted them on their shoulders and tried to smile. "We'll be tying up in a little while and you boys can go hunting for greens. Shawnee salad would make a wonderful supper, wouldn't it?"

The boys made faces, but Rachel knew that they'd be grateful for the tender dandelions and pokeweed and lamb's lettuce that made up their whole diet these days. If only the men could find meat, everyone's spirits might improve.

That evening, for the first time in weeks, they happened upon a buffalo. It was tough and the taste was so strong that it made Rachel wrinkle her nose, but not a morsel was left when supper was over. The next night they killed and ate a swan. All agreed it was the most delicious meat they had ever tasted.

Their hopes lifted by full bellies, the travelers journeyed on. They were sure the Big Salt Lick lay just around the next bend.

On the last day of March, they met a man named Richard Henderson and a party of surveyors marking the line between Virginia and North Carolina. Henderson had good news.

"You're very near the Big Salt Lick," he said. "It will be only a matter of days before you arrive." But he had no food for the hungry travelers. "There is a shipment of corn on the way from Boonesborough to the Big Salt Lick," he said. "Until then, perhaps Shawnee salad will—"

Rachel put her fingers in her ears. She never, never, never wanted to hear about Shawnee salad again.

It was Monday, April 24, 1780.

Four months and two days had passed since the Donelson flotilla had departed Fort Patrick Henry. They had traveled more than a thousand miles. Thirty-three of their companions had been lost to disease or drowning or Indians. Those that were left were exhausted and discouraged and near starvation.

The children didn't even bother asking "How much longer till

Replica of Fort Nashborough on the Cumberland River (Courtesy TSLA)

we get there?" It seemed that they would live on a boat for the rest of their lives.

The squawking of a red-tailed hawk made Rachel look up. High above, on bluffs overlooking the Cumberland River, she saw smoke. It was coming from the chimneys of a small cluster of log cabins.

At last, the travelers had arrived at Fort Nashborough near the Big Salt Lick—the place that would soon become Nashville, Tennessee.

For the first time in months, everyone was smiling. The people on the boats rushed ashore to greet husbands and sons and brothers. Joy mixed with sadness at the news of the many deaths among the river travelers. Mr. and Mrs. Peyton stood apart from the others. She wiped tears from his face as she spoke.

Captain Robertson and Colonel Donelson were both talking at once, words spilling out so fast that Rachel could scarcely take them in.

"Every last one of us made it," Robertson was saying, "though at times I had my doubts that we would. How was it with you, man?"

Rachel turned and went to find her brother William. There was no need to stay and listen to what her father had to say. She had lived every minute of the story he was about to tell.

25

(Just a few years later, Rachel would meet and fall in love with Andrew Jackson, who became the seventh President of the United States. Read their story in Chapter Four.)

BIBLIOGRAPHY

Davidson, Donald. *The Tennessee: The Old River Frontier to Secession*. Lanham, Md.: J. S. Sanders and Company, 1946.

Govan, Christine Noble. *Rachel Jackson—Tennessee Girl*. New York: Bobbs-Merrill Company, 1962.

Quarles, Robert T. and Robert H. White, eds. "Three Pioneer Tennessee Documents: Donelson's Journal." Tennessee Historical Commission, 1964.

Sioussat, St. George L., ed. "Selected Letters, 1846-56, from the Donelson Papers." *Tennessee Historical Magazine*, vol. 3 (1917): 257-291.

Spence, Richard Douglas. "John Donelson and the Opening of the Old Southwest." *Tennessee Historical Quarterly 50*, no. 3 (1991): 157-721.

Stone, Irving. *The President's Lady: A Novel About Rachel and Andrew Jackson*. Garden City, N. Y.: Doubleday, 1951.

Chapter Three

OLD MAN RIVER RUNS BACKWARDS

The Birth of Reelfoot Lake

—◦—

Once upon a time, almost 200 years ago, a tribe of Chickasaw Indians lived on a high bluff overlooking the mighty Mississippi River.

The chief who ruled the tribe had a heavy heart because his only son had been born with a horribly deformed foot. The boy didn't merely limp when he walked or ran; his body swung from side to side in a wild rolling motion. And so his people called him *Kalopin*, which in English means *reel foot*, or clubfoot.

Reelfoot became chief when his father died. He was a popular ruler, but he was often sad and lonely, for in his village he could not find even one young woman who stirred thoughts of love within him.

Reelfoot decided to travel south to where the Choctaw Indians lived. The Choctaws were famous for the wondrous beauty of their women. Reelfoot thought perhaps he could find a wife among their tribe.

He and his warriors floated down the great river in their canoes for many days. Late one evening, they arrived at a Choctaw village and cautiously drew near the council fire.

The flickering firelight cast its glow on the most beautiful woman Reelfoot had ever beheld. She was Princess Laughing Eyes, the chief's daughter. Her eyes and hair were as black as the night sky, and her smile made his heart turn somersaults.

The Choctaws welcomed their visitors. After they had feasted on roasted venison and smoked the peace pipe together, Reelfoot knelt before the old chief.

"Would you consent to give me your daughter's hand in marriage?" he asked.

"Marriage!" the old man said with surprise. "To you? Certainly not."

"But I am a rich and powerful Chickasaw leader," Reelfoot replied.

"No matter," said the chief. "My daughter will be given in wedlock only to a Choctaw chieftain. And even if you were a Choctaw, surely you do not think I would allow Laughing Eyes to marry a crippled man!"

The words hurt, but Reelfoot would not give up. "I will give you animal skins and pearls and other treasures if you will only give me the chance to court your daughter," he pleaded.

"No!" the old chief said. "Absolutely not."

Then the chief called on the Great Spirit, who warned Reelfoot with these words:

"DO NOT STEAL A WIFE FROM A NEIGHBORING TRIBE. IF YOU DO, I WILL CAUSE THE EARTH TO ROCK AND THE RIVER TO SWALLOW UP YOUR PEOPLE AND BURY THEM IN A WATERY GRAVE."

Reelfoot was so frightened that he and his men returned home. Many months passed, but he could not forget the beautiful princess.

When winter came, he and his warriors again boarded their canoes and floated downriver. In the dead of night, they crept into the Choctaw village and captured Laughing Eyes.

"Please, Reelfoot, don't do this," the princess begged as he led her toward the river. "You heard what the Great Spirit said when you visited my village many months ago."

"I heard, but I don't care," Reelfoot replied. "My love for you is greater than my fear of the Great Spirit. We will return to my home and you will become my wife."

He helped the princess into his canoe and began paddling north with all his might.

There was great rejoicing when Reelfoot and Laughing Eyes reached the Chickasaw village. The people prepared a great wedding festival. They beat upon kettledrums and tom-toms as the marriage ceremony began.

Suddenly, the earth began to roll in rhythm to the music. Huge cracks split the land. The Chickasaws reeled and staggered. Some of them tried to flee to the hills, but the ground shook so violently that they were knocked off their feet.

Then the Great Spirit stamped his foot in anger and the people fell into the gigantic hole that was formed in the earth. The mighty Mississippi River turned backwards over its course, running uphill and out of its banks to fill the hole. The tribe was buried beneath its stormy waters.

Where Reelfoot and his people once lived, a beautiful lake was formed.

Those who look carefully beneath its waters can see the glint of royal beads. And if they look closely enough, they can sometimes glimpse the lovely face of Princess Laughing Eyes.

That's one story of how Tennessee's Reelfoot Lake came to be. But the next story is the one that most people today believe is true.

Along the Mississippi River, where the states of Arkansas, Kentucky, Missouri, and Tennessee meet, lies the New Madrid Fault. A *fault* is a crack in the earth's surface. When the hot liquid that lies beneath the surface moves, it causes rocks on one side of the fault to push against rocks on the other side. Pressure builds. When the pressure is too strong, the rocks buckle and break, releasing stored energy.

When that happens, an earthquake occurs. Some earthquakes are hardly noticeable and cause no damage. Others are disastrous to people and property.

The town of New Madrid, Missouri, lies along the New Madrid Fault, just across the Mississippi River from northwest Tennessee. In December 1811, a powerful earthquake occurred in New Madrid. Another violent quake took place there in late January 1812 and a third only a couple of weeks afterwards.

About 200 people lived in New Madrid during that time. Most of what people today know about those earthquakes comes from stories the town residents told.

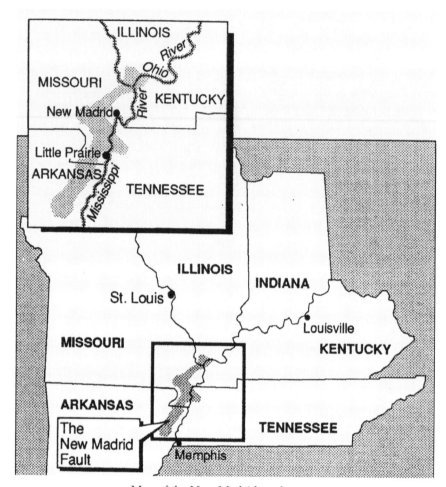

Map of the New Madrid quake zone

"There was the most awful noise," one resident said. "It sounded like hoarse and vibrating thunder. There was the crack of falling trees, the roaring of the river, and total darkness filled with a thick vapor that smelled of sulfur."

Another terrified person described how the earth shook. "It was as if I stood upon something that swayed from side to side and sank and rose with irregular motions. I was thrown down twelve times trying to climb the front steps of my house to rescue the baby."

One man told of "huge circular holes in the earth, spewing forth sand and a black substance like coal."

Still another resident spoke of "scores of people running about, screaming and yelling and wringing their hands. No pencil can paint the distress of the inhabitants of New Madrid."

The Mississippi River was filled with boat traffic when the earth exploded, and some of the most vivid descriptions come from people who were on the water.

"I was awakened from a sound sleep by a most tremendous noise," one boatman wrote. "The boat gave a lurch, as if it had been lifted from the water and dropped abruptly. All nature seemed to be running into chaos. Ducks and geese and other wildfowl screamed and flocked to settle on our boats. Smaller birds landed and perched on people's heads and shoulders."

Another boatman told of how the river "foamed up like the water in a boiling cauldron . . . collapsing the river banks in large columns and throwing thousands of fish up to die on dry land."

Many people described the hundreds of uprooted trees that clogged the river. Some claimed that the Mississippi River actually ran backwards for several days, but scientists today think that the mighty river probably never really ran upstream. It is more likely that the sudden impact of trees, dirt, and other debris caused huge swells in the river, and that those swells produced a tidal-wave effect that made it look like the river was running backwards.

In modern times, scientists called *seismologists* are able to calculate the power of earthquakes. Using an instrument known as the *seismograph*, they can measure and describe an earthquake's severity in comparison with other earthquakes.

There were no seismologists or seismographs in the early 1800s, but newspaper accounts from all over the United States and eyewitness descriptions have led scientists and historians to believe that the New Madrid earthquakes are the most powerful in the recorded history of North America.

Aftershocks, violent shakings that follow an earthquake, were felt as far south as the Gulf of Mexico and as far north as Canada. Tremors shook buildings on the Atlantic coast from Connecticut to Georgia. All across the United States, plaster cracked, clocks stopped, and steeple bells rang.

It has been estimated that the New Madrid earthquakes were felt over nearly a million square miles!

No one knows for sure how many people were killed by the

New Madrid earthquakes. Only a few of those who lived in towns along the river died, but many more perished on the Mississippi River.

Witnesses told of large boats completely buried beneath gigantic waves. Others described the screams and cries of men whose boats were dashed against the riverbanks.

"We made no effort to find out how many had been killed," one boatman said. "We saw the dead bodies of several drowned persons floating in the river."

Because the Indians who lived in the area had no written language, it is impossible to know how many of them the earthquakes killed.

The quakes drastically changed the way the land looked. On the Mississippi River, great numbers of sandbars and islands disappeared and new ones formed where none were before.

On both sides of the river, cracks too wide to be crossed on horseback split the earth. More than 150,000 acres of timber were destroyed. Farmland became swamps. Streams changed courses. Huge tracts of forest sank, leaving treetops level with the surrounding earth. And as some land sank and other land was raised up, ponds and lakes were formed.

That's how Tennessee's Reelfoot Lake was born.

For several years after the earthquakes, the area around the lake remained primarily Indian country. White explorers and settlers began moving into the area in small numbers in the 1820s.

As years passed and pioneers pushed westward through Tennessee in the never-ending search for adventure and fertile cropland, the population around Reelfoot Lake grew.

The Chickasaws were forced off the land in 1837 in the journey to Oklahoma now known as the Trail of Tears. Plantation owners settled on the rich bottomland near the Mississippi River. Folks who settled east of the lake scratched out a meager living hunting and fishing.

Disagreements over who actually owned Reelfoot Lake led to violence in the early 1900s.

Beginning in 1907, the West Tennessee Land Company quietly began purchasing old land claims dating back to the years before Reelfoot Lake was formed. The company planned to drain the lake and convert it to farmland. When folks who lived in the area discovered those plans, they were upset.

"No!" they cried. "This land is public property. It belongs to everyone. It's wrong to buy or sell it."

"Oh, but you're mistaken," company officials argued. "Our lawyers have researched land titles from many years back. You people don't own the lake—you've just been using it for free. We have every right to purchase this lake and do what we wish with it."

"But we've hunted these woods and fished these waters all our lives," the lake people argued. "Our parents and grandparents did, too. You have no right to take it from us."

"We'll see about that," came the reply. "Before long, your favorite fishing spot will be growing thousands of acres of cotton."

Lake residents reacted with violence in 1908. Night Riders—armed men wearing masks and gowns—terrorized and attacked land company officials and their supporters. One of the officials was murdered; another escaped death by hiding all night under a

Duck hunters on Reelfoot Lake
(Courtesy TSLA)

cypress log in a swamp.

More than 100 men were arrested and accused of being Night Riders, but the cases against them were eventually dropped. Most of the public sided with the lake people instead of the land company.

In 1914 the state of Tennessee acquired ownership of Reelfoot Lake. Eleven years later, the state also purchased the land surrounding the lake and established Reelfoot Lake Park and Fish and Game Preserve.

Today, Reelfoot Lake's 25,000 acres are a paradise for hunters, fishermen, and nature lovers. Visitors from all over the United States travel to northwest Tennessee to partake of its "otherworld loveliness."

The lake's shallow waters, which average only six feet in depth, make it the nation's most abundant natural fish hatchery. More than five dozen varieties of fish—most notably largemouth bass, bream, and crappie—make their homes near the cypress stumps and lily pads that dot the lake.

While most lakes in the United States average 180 pounds of fish per acre, Reelfoot averages more than 1,200 pounds per acre. Reelfoot is the only lake in the country where commercial fishing is legal. On a good day, a persistent fisherman might catch as many as 300 crappie and an ice chest full of platter-sized bluegill.

And Reelfoot is home to almost every species of shore and wading bird native to North America, including a large number of bald eagles that migrate to the lake each winter to nest in the giant cypress trees.

Thousands of ducks and geese draw hunters to the area in winter, as do—in their proper seasons—deer, turkey, quail, rabbit, and squirrel.

For those who aren't interested in hunting or fishing, there is plenty to do. A three-mile boardwalk over the cypress wetlands, and scenic guided boat cruises give visitors a chance to study the lake up close. Numerous motels and lodges, as well as picnic areas, playgrounds, tennis courts, ball fields, and swimming pools add to Reelfoot Lake's popularity as a vacation destination.

Many visitors come back again and again, grateful that Chief Reelfoot ignored the warning not to steal a wife from a neighboring tribe.

Cypress trees on Reelfoot Lake
(Courtesy TSLA)

BIBLIOGRAPHY

Harshaw, Lou as told by Juanita Clifton. *Reelfoot & the New Madrid Quake.* Asheville, N. C.: Victor Books, 1980.

Logsdon, David R. *I Was There in the New Madrid Earthquakes of 1811-12.* by the author, 1990.

Natural Disasters—Earthquakes. New York: Aladdin Books, 1992.

Penick, James Jr. *The New Madrid Earthquakes of 1811-12.* Columbia: University of Missouri Press, 1976.

Simon, Seymour. *Earthquakes.* New York: Morrow Jr. Books, 1991.

Sipiera, Paul P. *Earthquakes.* Danbury, Conn.: Grolier Publishing Company, 1998.

Vanderwood, Paul J. *Night Riders of Reelfoot Lake.* Memphis: Memphis State University Press, 1969.

Chapter Four

CALLING THE WHITE HOUSE HOME

Three Tennessee Presidents

Tennessee has sent three Presidents to the White House—more than any state except for Virginia, New York, and Ohio.

All three Tennessee Presidents served during the nineteenth century. Two of them had the same first name and the same initials. Two were born in a log cabin. Two were lawyers. Two had no children of their own. Two never went to college. Two served only one term in office. None of the three was born in Tennessee, but all of them considered themselves Tennesseans.

Just who were these men who called the White House "home"? Read on. . . .

ANDREW JACKSON
Old Hickory

When Andrew Jackson was born on March 15, 1767, his widowed mother did not know that he would grow up to become an attorney and a prosperous landowner. She did not know that he would fight in two wars against Great Britain. She did not know that he would marry the same woman twice. And she did not know that he would become the seventh President of the United States—the first President born in a log cabin.

She knew, as she lay cradling her newborn son in her arms, only

Chapter 1

Statue on North Carolina Capitol grounds, Raleigh
(Photo by Dick Rand)

that life for this child and his brothers was not going to be easy.

Two years earlier, Elizabeth Jackson and her husband, Andrew, along with their young sons, Hugh and Robert, had come to the American colonies from Ireland. They worked hard building a crude cabin and farming the small piece of rocky land they bought in the Waxhaw settlement on the border of North and South Carolina.

They were looking forward to the birth of their third child.

But their dreams ended in tragedy. A week before the baby was born, Mr. Jackson died of a heart attack, leaving his wife to raise their two older boys and baby Andrew all by herself.

When young Andrew Jackson turned five years old, his mother enrolled him in school. Although he preferred sports and fistfights to studying, he was a bright student who learned quickly.

He was soon chosen as a "public reader" to read newspaper items aloud to illiterate members of the community. "I was selected to read as often as any grown man," he later recalled. Some stories say that when he was nine years old, he stood on a chair and read the newly adopted Declaration of Independence to his neighbors.

Though the Carolinas were still British colonies, Jackson and his family considered themselves Americans. After the Revolutionary War began, both Hugh and Robert enrolled in the South Carolina militia. Hugh was killed in battle. As the war drew closer to the Carolinas, Andrew begged his mother to allow him to enlist. She finally consented.

Andrew Jackson was only thirteen years old when he became a soldier.

Both Robert and Andrew were captured by the British Army in 1781. Soon after they were taken prisoner, the commanding officer ordered Andrew to scrub his muddy boots.

"I am a prisoner of war, not a servant!" Andrew replied with indignation.

With that, the angry officer drew his sword and swung it at the boy, slicing a deep cut in Andrew's face and head and slashing his hand to the bone. Jackson proudly carried those scars for the rest of his life.

He carried some emotional scars, too. Robert died of smallpox while he was a prisoner of war. And a few months later, their mother, Elizabeth, died, leaving fourteen-year-old Andrew Jackson an orphan, totally alone in the world.

When the war was over, Jackson drifted into bad habits. He squandered his small inheritance on horse racing, cockfighting, and card playing.

In those days, free public schools did not exist. Parents had to pay to educate their children. Anyone who could read and write could be a teacher, and that's what Jackson did after his money ran out.

When he grew tired of teaching, he headed to Western North Carolina. He worked as a lawyer's apprentice and soon learned enough law to become a licensed attorney. At the age of twenty, he decided to seek his fortune across the Appalachian Mountains, in Tennessee.

Jackson arrived in Nashville in 1788. He established a successful law practice and began making money buying and selling land. He rented a room in a boarding house owned by the widow of John Donelson, one of the founders of Nashville.

Mrs. Donelson's daughter Rachel lived at the boarding house and helped her mother. Rachel was a beautiful, dark-eyed young woman whose unhappy marriage to Lewis Robards had ended in separation. She and Jackson struck up a friendship that gradually evolved into romance.

When Rachel heard that her husband had published a divorce notice in the newspaper, she and Jackson made plans to wed. They were married in Natchez, Mississippi, in August 1791 and lived happily together for the next two years.

Then they learned of some scandalous news.

Lewis Robards had never actually divorced Rachel. He had only advertised his intent to divorce. That made Rachel a *bigamist*—a person married to more than one spouse at the same time. She and Jackson were devastated by the news. They had violated one of society's strongest legal and moral codes without even knowing it.

They did the only thing they could do under the circumstances. After Rachel received official divorce papers from Robards, she and Jackson married again, this time in January 1794. That marriage was to endure for almost forty years.

In 1796 Tennessee became the sixteenth state to join the Union. Andrew Jackson was elected to be Tennessee's first member of the U.S. House of Representatives. In 1797 he was chosen to serve in the U.S. Senate. But life in the nation's capital did not suit Jackson. He resigned his position and headed home to Tennessee.

Jackson continued to be involved in business. He owned a general store. He also bought and sold land, including acreage he purchased east of Nashville, where he and Rachel built a home they named "The Hermitage."

One of Jackson's favorite hobbies was horse racing. He built fine stables and a racetrack. He made a great deal of money raising and betting on horses.

That hobby was the cause of one of the most infamous incidents in Jackson's life. In a dispute over a horse race, Jackson challenged a man named Charles Dickinson to a duel. Dickinson had also made insulting remarks about Rachel's character and reputation, which infuriated the hot-tempered Jackson.

Dueling was illegal in Tennessee, so the two men agreed that the gunfight would be held just over the state line, in Kentucky. When they met on the dueling grounds, Jackson was wearing a loose-fitting coat over his tall, thin body. Dickinson fired first after the signal to shoot was given, aiming for Jackson's heart. His bullet lodged in Jackson's lung instead.

Jackson had deliberately waited for Dickinson to take his shot. Now it was his turn.

He cocked his pistol's hammer and pulled the trigger, but nothing happened. Many of the onlookers thought that meant his turn was over, but that's not what Jackson thought. He cocked and pulled the trigger again, and this time the gun fired. The bullet hit Dickinson in the belly. He died a few hours later, and though Jackson eventually recovered from his wound, he carried Dickinson's bullet in his lung for the rest of his life.

It was during the War of 1812, against Great Britain, that Jackson earned the nickname "Old Hickory" and became a national hero.

"General Jackson is good to us," one of his soldiers once remarked.

"Yes, and he's tough as a hickory tree," another replied. The nickname stuck.

In 1814 in Alabama, Jackson and his men fought and defeated the Creek Indians who had allied themselves with the British. During the Battle of Horseshoe Bend, American soldiers found an Indian baby clutched in the arms of his dead mother.

Jackson, perhaps remembering that he himself had been orphaned during a war, asked that the child be sent to The Hermitage so that Rachel could care for him. The boy's name was Lyncoya. The Jacksons raised him and one of Rachel's nephews (whom they named Andrew Jr.) as though they were their own sons.

At the Battle of New Orleans, in January 1815, Jackson gained national fame when his 5,000 ragtag troops soundly defeated a British army of 8,000 men. More than 300 British soldiers were killed. Hundreds more were captured. Less than a dozen Americans lost their lives.

Jackson returned to Tennessee a hero.

He hoped to settle down to a quiet life at The Hermitage with his family. But that was not to be. He served another term as U.S. Senator. Then, in 1824, his political supporters urged him to seek a much bigger office. They wanted him to run for President of the United States. Reluctantly, Jackson agreed.

Jackson won more votes in the election of 1824 than any other candidate, but he did not receive the majority of electoral votes. That meant that the House of Representatives had to choose the

General Jackson at the Battle of New Orleans
(Courtesy TSLA)

next President. Instead of Jackson, they chose John Quincy Adams. "Corruption!" Jackson cried. "Next time, I won't be defeated."

He was right. In 1828 he ran for President again. He won by a landslide, but victory came with a huge price. The practice of *mudslinging*—saying negative things, often false or superficial, about a political opponent—played a big part in the campaign. Most of the mudslinging was aimed at Jackson and Rachel.

Opponents talked about his hot temper and his lack of formal education. They called him a murderer and a wife stealer.

Even worse things were said about Rachel. Jackson's enemies made fun of her plump figure and dowdy clothes. They called her "unrefined" and pointed out that she often smoked cigars or a pipe. Most hurtful of all, they reminded voters that Rachel had once been married to two men at the same time.

Although Jackson tried to shield Rachel from the negative things that were said during the campaign, he was not successful. Learning of them filled her with humiliation and shame.

Rachel Donelson Jackson would never live in the White House. On December 22, 1828, just a few weeks after her husband's victory, she suffered a heart attack and died. She was buried on Christmas Eve in the flower garden at The Hermitage, dressed in the gown she was to have worn at the inaugural ball.

Heartbroken, Jackson made the long trip to Washington, D.C., to be sworn in as President in March 1829. While the inauguration ceremony itself was dignified, the party that followed was like nothing Washington Society had ever seen.

More than 20,000 well-wishers followed Jackson from the Capitol to the White House. They were thrilled that an "ordinary American" had finally been elected to the highest office in the country, and they planned to celebrate with gusto.

Men in muddy boots climbed through White House windows and stood on silk-covered furniture to get a better look at Old Hickory. They spit tobacco juice on the expensive carpets and quickly devoured the 1,400-pound wheel of cheese that had been ordered for the occasion. Fistfights broke out every few minutes. Most of the presidential china and fine crystal was broken.

MRS. RACHEL JACKSON   GENERAL ANDREW JACKSON

Mrs. Jackson's likeness is from the miniature that General Jackson wore every day until his death. His is from the well-known military portrait by Earle.

Cameo portraits of Rachel and Andrew Jackson
(Courtesy TSLA)

Jackson standing on the driveway of the Hermitage. Rachel's grave is on the right in the picture. (Courtesy TSLA)

Jackson finally escaped the crowd by sneaking out the back door. The White House staff moved tubs of punch to the Executive Mansion's lawn to lure the revelers outside. Then they locked all the doors and windows.

The administration of the common man had begun. It was to be called the "Age of Jackson"—a term which showed that the nation's first frontier President believed that ordinary people had enough sense to make decisions for themselves and to let their voices be heard in government.

In the two terms that Jackson served as President, 1829-1837, he did things that pleased some people and things that angered others. He fired government workers who did not support him, and replaced them with his friends. He ordered federal troops to remove Indians from the southeastern part of the United States to lands west of the Mississippi River, the journey that became known as the Trail of Tears. He dissolved the Bank of the United States. He paid off the national debt. He stood up to South Carolina's effort to ignore federal laws. He established diplomatic relations with the newly formed Republic of Texas.

And at the end of his eight years as President, Andrew Jackson was tired.

Ill with tuberculosis and still grief stricken over Rachel's death, Jackson returned to The Hermitage, where he spent his days riding horses and supervising his plantation. He continued his interest in politics and supported the presidential candidacies of Martin Van Buren and fellow Tennessean James K. Polk.

On June 8, 1845, at the age of seventy-eight, Jackson died in his bed at the Hermitage. He was buried next to his beloved Rachel.

◦

JAMES K. POLK
Young Hickory

Small and frail, Jimmy Polk was seldom able to run and play with other boys. Farm chores exhausted him. He was not even healthy enough to go to school. But he had a strong mind and strong ambition—ambition that eventually led him to become the eleventh President of the United States.

James K. Polk was born on November 2, 1795, on a farm near Pineville, North Carolina. Like the Jacksons, his parents, Samuel and Jane Knox Polk, were Irish immigrants. Like Jackson, Polk lived in a log cabin. But unlike the Jacksons, the Polks were a well-to-do and prominent family.

Jimmy was the oldest of ten brothers and sisters. When he was ten years old, his father decided to move the family from North Carolina to Middle Tennessee. Even though Jimmy's health was poor, he walked the entire 500-mile trip because there was no room in the family's wagon for anyone except the babies.

The Polks settled on land near Columbia, Tennessee, where they soon became one of the wealthiest families in the area.

When he was sixteen years old, Jimmy's medical problem was diagnosed as gallstones. His doctor suggested that he travel to Danville, Kentucky, to have the stones removed by a renowned surgeon who practiced there.

Jimmy and his father made the grueling ride on horseback to Kentucky. In the days before anesthesia, surgical patients were often given a swig of whisky to drink and a bullet to bite on. Then they were held down by force while the surgeon operated on them.

That's how Jimmy had his gallstones removed.

It took several weeks of recovery after the operation before he was well enough to return to Tennessee, but he proudly carried a bottle containing the stones home with him.

The surgery made a big difference in Jimmy's health. For the first time in his life, he felt like going to school rather than being tutored at home. He attended private academies near Columbia for two years and then enrolled in the University of North Carolina at Chapel Hill in 1815. He graduated at the top of his class three years later. He was the only one of Tennessee's three Presidents who attended college.

Polk, who now insisted on being called "James" rather than "Jimmy," studied law with famous Nashville attorney Felix Grundy and opened his own law practice in Columbia in 1820. His interest in government and politics continued to grow. He served as chief clerk of the Tennessee State Senate, and in 1823 he was elected a member of the Tennessee House of Representatives.

It looked like Polk was on his way to a successful political career, and his friend Andrew Jackson had some advice for him.

"What you need to do," Jackson told Polk, "is to stop dallying about and get married."

"There's a young woman in Murfreesboro who is the sister of one of my former schoolmates," Polk said. "I've known her since she was eleven years old, and we've always liked each other. Her name is Sarah Childress. Do you know her?"

Jackson smiled and nodded. "Yes, indeed. And I think she'd be the perfect wife. She's wealthy, intelligent, and good-looking. She can't help but advance your political career."

Jackson was right about Sarah. Daughter of one of the wealthiest families in Murfreesboro, she had been provided a formal education far beyond that of most young women of her time. She was cultured, sophisticated, and very well read. With dark hair and eyes and an olive complexion, she was stunningly beautiful.

And Sarah Childress was as smitten with James K. Polk as he was with her.

They courted for several months. When Polk proposed marriage, Sarah happily consented. They were married on New Year's Day of 1824 at the Childress plantation in Murfreesboro.

A few months earlier Polk had been elected to his first political office—a seat in the Tennessee House of Representatives. One of the first choices he had to make was whether to support Andrew Jackson's bid for the U.S. Senate. He supported Jackson, and from that time forward, the men were close friends and political allies—so close, in fact, that Polk was sometimes called "Young Hickory."

Polk's success in politics grew. In 1825 he was elected to the U.S. House of Representatives. He served seven terms there and was eventually named Speaker of the House, where he used his influence to help further President Andrew Jackson's policies.

He was elected governor of Tennessee in 1839 but was defeated for that office in the following two elections. He feared his political career might be at an end.

He was wrong.

When the Democratic Party could not agree on a choice for its presidential nominee in 1844, they began to consider Polk. He was well educated. He had experience at many levels of government. And he had something even more important—he had the support of his old friend Andrew Jackson.

Polk became the Democratic Party's nominee for President. He was the first "dark horse" candidate in U.S. history. Not many people knew who he was.

His opponent, Henry Clay, used the fact that Polk was an unknown as a slogan in his campaign against him. "Who is James K. Polk?" he and his supporters asked.

They soon found out. Polk narrowly defeated Clay in the race. At age forty-nine, he became the youngest person up to that time to be elected President.

By his side was one of the ablest assistants any President had ever had—his wife, Sarah. Because the Polks had no children to occupy Sarah's time, and because she was fascinated with politics and current events, she became her husband's personal secretary and advisor.

She spent hours every day going through stacks of newspapers, clipping articles she thought he should read. She helped him write letters and practice his speeches. She traveled about the country with him. She often sat in the ladies' gallery in the House of Representatives, taking notes as she watched the proceedings.

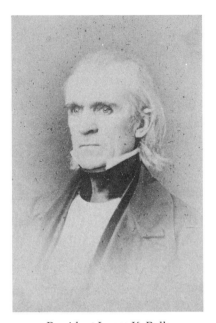

President James K. Polk
(Courtesy TSLA)

Sarah Childress Polk
(Courtesy TSLA)

As First Lady, Sarah Polk entertained differently than most of the Presidents' wives had in the past. She did not serve refreshments at White House receptions because she believed that conversation rather than food should be the focus of those functions. And because of her strict religious background, she did not allow alcohol, card playing, or dancing at the White House.

When the Polks entered the room at their own inaugural ball, the music and dancing immediately came to a halt. It did not resume again until the couple had shaken hands with all their guests and departed.

Sarah was so caught up in the world of politics that she sometimes forgot to eat at the White House dinners she hosted. She always preferred serious conversation with the men to social chitchat with their wives. No First Lady before and very few since played such an active role in helping run the country.

Sarah Polk began two traditions that are still carried on in modern times.

The first is an annual Thanksgiving dinner for government officials. The second is the playing of "Hail to the Chief" when the President enters the room at an important event. Sarah wrote that song for her husband because she feared his small size would keep him from being noticed if his appearance was not accompanied by music.

One of Polk's campaign promises was that he would not seek reelection. Some historians have called him the nation's greatest one-term President. He was without a doubt one of the hardest-working men to ever serve in that office.

"No President who performs his duty faithfully and conscientiously can have any leisure," Polk once said.

He was true to his word. He welcomed every visitor who wished to discuss any type of government business with him. He required that all his department heads turn in daily reports, which he studied carefully. He often worked so hard that he made himself sick.

Polk's major goal as President was to acquire more land for the United States. He believed in *Manifest Destiny*—the idea that it was right and proper for the nation to control the North American continent from the Atlantic Ocean to the Pacific.

He bargained with the British for the Oregon territory, which was made up of modern-day Oregon, Washington, Idaho, Montana, and parts of western Canada.

And in a war with Mexico from 1846-1848, a conflict that is often called "Mr. Polk's War," he acquired Texas, California, Utah, Nevada, and parts of six other states in exchange for $15,000,000.

Following that war, James K. Polk governed a country that spread from ocean to ocean. He had almost doubled the size of the United States and had gained all the territory that would make up the first forty-eight states. Ironically, he never set foot on any of the land he helped acquire.

Other important things happened while Polk was President. He lowered the import tariff and reorganized the U.S. Treasury. The first U.S. postage stamp was used to mail a letter. Gold was discovered in California. The U.S. Naval Academy and the Smithsonian Institution were built.

At the end of it all, Polk was worn out. Shortly before he left office, he and Sarah bought a beautiful mansion in Nashville that they named "Polk Place." They looked forward to their retirement there.

Polk Place, Nashville. The Polks' graves, pictured at right, were later moved to the grounds of the Tennessee Capitol. (Courtesy TSLA)

But Polk became ill on a farewell trip from Washington back to Tennessee. He contracted cholera, an intestinal disease that causes severe diarrhea.

Less than three months after he left office, he died. He was fifty-three years old.

Sarah lived at Polk Place for her remaining forty-two years, dressed always in black as a sign of mourning for her husband. During the Civil War she refused to take sides with either the Union or the Confederacy. She insisted that Polk Place be neutral ground, and she graciously received guests from both armies there.

Sarah died in 1891 and was buried beside James in the garden at Polk Place. In 1893 their graves were moved to the grounds of the Tennessee State Capitol, where they remain.

Polk Place is no longer standing, but James K. Polk's ancestral home in Columbia, Tennessee, has been preserved by the state as a museum honoring the eleventh President of the United States.

ANDREW JOHNSON
The Tennessee Tailor

Some Americans thought that President Andrew Johnson, the seventeenth President of the United States, was a hero. Others called him a traitor. He has gone down in history not so much for what he did but for what almost happened to him. He was almost kicked out of office.

Andrew Johnson was born on December 29, 1808, in Raleigh, North Carolina, to poor, illiterate parents. Unlike Presidents Jackson and Polk, Johnson wasn't born in a log cabin. He was born in a run-down clapboard shack.

Andrew barely knew his father. Jacob Johnson died of a heart attack when Andrew was only three years old, leaving Polly Johnson to raise Andrew and his older brother William alone.

Unlike Andrew Jackson and James K. Polk, Andrew Johnson never spent a day of his life in a classroom. His mother worked as a washerwoman and could not afford to send him to school. Because she could neither read nor write, she could not teach him those skills at home.

In those days, boys who had little or no education were often apprenticed to craftsmen to learn a skill. In exchange for their upkeep and for being taught a trade, the boys were expected to work for their employer for seven years. Polly bound her sons over to a tailor in Raleigh when Andrew was just nine years old.

Andrew Johnson's birthplace, Raleigh, N.C.
(Photo by Dick Rand)

The young apprentices spent long hours sitting cross-legged on a workbench in the dreary tailor shop, cutting and sewing cloth. Some of the boys grew restless and bored. But not Andrew Johnson. Something magical was happening to him while he worked.

To keep the boys' minds occupied while they sewed, public-spirited citizens often came to the tailor shop to read aloud to the workers. Sometimes they read newspapers. Other times they read books. Occasionally they read speeches by famous orators. Andrew was fascinated by the topics that the men who visited the shop read and discussed.

More than anything, he wanted to read about events and ideas himself. He persuaded his boss to teach him the alphabet. Some of the volunteer readers and the older boys in the shop helped him sound out simple words. One man gave him books to take home at night.

That's how Andrew Johnson taught himself to read. His world would never be the same again.

When he was sixteen years old, Johnson ran away. He was tired of working as a tailor's apprentice and wanted to see the world. But when he learned that his mother and stepfather wanted to move west of the Appalachian Mountains, he returned to Raleigh to help them.

The family loaded a wagon with their meager possessions, hitched it to a blind horse, and headed for Tennessee. They settled in a beautiful valley near the bustling little town of Greeneville. That's where seventeen-year-old Andrew Johnson fell in love with sixteen-year-old Eliza McCardle.

One story says that the first time Eliza saw Andrew, she whispered to her friends, "There goes my beau, girls, mark it!"

And soon after Andrew saw Eliza for the first time, he told his mother, "I've found the girl I'm going to marry."

Less than a year later, on May 17, 1827, Andrew and Eliza were wed. Their rented two-room cottage served both as a tailor shop and a home, the home where Eliza tutored her young husband in the basics of arithmetic and writing.

The tailor business grew, and so did the Johnson family. Four children were born during Andrew and Eliza's first eight years of marriage. A fifth child was born much later—in 1852.

Remembering his days as a teenage apprentice, Johnson hired a person to read newspapers, books, and speeches aloud to him while he worked at his sewing. His tailor shop became a gathering place for many of the men in town who were interested in discussing politics.

"Andrew, why don't you consider running for public office?" one of his friends asked.

"Me? Why I'd never have a chance of being elected," Johnson replied.

"I think you're wrong," another man said. "You know just about everything there is to know about current events, and you're a powerful speaker."

"But I have no formal education. I'm just a simple tailor. Why would voters choose someone like me?" Johnson asked.

"Because you're one of them. Folks around here know you'll look after the interests of the common people instead of catering to those of wealth and privilege. Greeneville needs a fellow like you. Won't you at least consider running for town council?"

"I guess it can't hurt to try," Johnson replied. His political career had begun.

Andrew Johnson was elected to the Greeneville Town Council in 1828. Two years later, voters chose him mayor of Greeneville. After that, he won a seat in the state legislature. He served first in the Tennessee House of Representatives and then in the Senate.

Now his eyes turned toward a bigger prize—the United States Congress.

In 1842, the East Tennessee tailor-politician was elected to the U.S. House of Representatives, where he served for ten years.

Then it was back to Tennessee, where he served two terms as governor. Johnson was often called "the mechanic governor" because he continued to look after the interests of common people. During his terms as governor, he helped establish public schools and libraries so that all the people could enjoy the benefits of education.

In 1857 Johnson returned to Washington, D.C., to serve in the U.S. Senate. It was a time when trouble was brewing between the North and the South—trouble that would soon lead to the Civil War.

Abraham Lincoln was elected President of the United States in 1860. Some of the Southern states believed he would put an end to slavery. To keep that from happening, those states seceded, or withdrew, from the Union.

Eventually, eleven states seceded and formed the Confederate States of America. Andrew Johnson's Tennessee was number eleven. One by one, the U.S. Senators from those states resigned their seats. Twenty-one went home to the South.

Only one stayed—Andrew Johnson.

Although Johnson was not against slavery, he was against secession. "Those who want to secede are traitors against the federal government," he said. "Were I the President of the United States . . . I would execute them!"

Johnson's speech made him popular with Northerners. But most of the people in Tennessee did not like it. They called Johnson a "traitor to the South."

After the Civil War started, President Lincoln appointed Johnson military governor of Tennessee. His job was to support the Union Army and to restore the authority of the federal government in the state. His actions made him even more unpopular with many Tennesseans.

But Lincoln admired the job Johnson did. He asked him to be

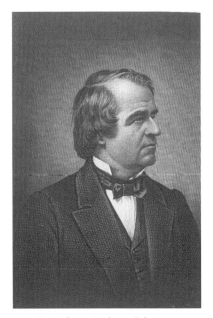

President Andrew Johnson
(Courtesy TSLA)

Eliza McCardle Johnson
(Courtesy TSLA)

his running mate in the election of 1864. The Lincoln-Johnson ticket won, and on March 4, 1865, Andrew Johnson was sworn in as Vice President. But he would not have that job for long.

Just a few weeks later, only days after the Civil War came to an end, President Lincoln was assassinated. Andrew Johnson became President of the United States.

Johnson was anxious for his family to join him in Washington, D.C., but he worried about them as they made the long journey through the hostile South. He was relieved when they made the trip safely and moved into the White House.

Ill with tuberculosis and grief stricken over her oldest son's death, Eliza Johnson was not well enough to serve as First Lady. She asked her daughter Martha to take the job instead.

"We are plain people from the mountains of Tennessee," Martha said as she accepted the job. "I trust too much will not be expected of us."

Martha was a most unusual First Lady. She insisted on doing most of the cleaning and other housework herself. She sewed her own calico dresses. She grazed two jersey cows on the White House lawn so the family could have fresh milk. She even churned her own butter.

Meanwhile, her father faced the huge task of putting the country back together after the terrible war that had ripped it apart.

More than 600,000 people had been killed in the Civil War. The South was in ruins. Johnson, like Lincoln, wanted to show compassion and forgiveness to the people of the South.

But many members of Congress did not. A group of Congressmen known as "Radical Republicans" had no interest in healing the nation's wounds. They wanted to inflict harsh punishments on the former Confederate states.

When Johnson would not go along with their plans, the House of Representatives impeached him, which means that they wanted to remove him from office. His trial was held in the U.S. Senate. He was found not guilty by just one vote.

He would remain President, but a very unpopular one.

Many important things happened during the four years Andrew Johnson was President. The thirteenth, fourteenth, and fifteenth amendments were added to the U.S. Constitution. Those amend-

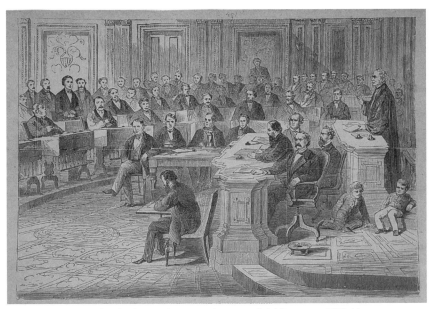

Sketch of Johnson's impeachment trial (Courtesy TSLA)

ments outlawed slavery, bestowed citizenship on the former slaves, and gave black men the right to vote.

The territory of Alaska was purchased from Russia during Johnson's presidency. And Johnson pardoned all of the Confederate leaders.

He was not nominated to run for President in 1868. When his term of office ended, Johnson quietly headed back to Greeneville. There, he spent time repairing the family home, which had been used as a Confederate hospital during the Civil War. He helped nurse the sick during an outbreak of cholera. And he became involved again in politics.

In 1875, Andrew Johnson did something that no former President had ever done before and no former President has done since. He was elected to the U.S. Senate. Much to his surprise, he was welcomed with cheers and applause. But just a few months later, on July 31, he suffered a stroke and died. He was sixty-seven years old.

"When I die I desire no better winding sheet than the Stars and Stripes, and no softer pillow than the Constitution of my country," Johnson had once said. He got his wish. He was buried on a hill overlooking Greeneville, his body wrapped in an American flag and his head resting on a copy of the U.S. Constitution.

His grave, house, and shop are now part of the Andrew Johnson National Historic Site in Greeneville, a little town proud to be the home of the Tennessee tailor who became the seventeenth President of the United States.

BIBLIOGRAPHY

Bausum, Ann and George W. Bush. *Our Country's Presidents*. Washington, D.C.: National Geographic Society, 2001.

Cleveland, Will and Mark Alvarez. *Yo, Millard Fillmore!: And All Those Other Presidents You Don't Know*. Brookfield, Conn.: Millbrook Press, 1997.

Durwood, Thomas A. and Cathy East Dubowski. *Andrew Johnson: Rebuilding the Union*. edited by Richard Gallin. Parsippany, N. J.: Silver Burdett, 1991.

Gormley, Beatrice. *First Ladies: Women Who Called the White House Home*. New York: Scholastic, 1997.

Judson, Karen. *Andrew Jackson*. Berkeley Heights, N. J.: Enslow Publishers, 1997.

Klapthor, Margaret Brown and Helen Claire Duprey Bullock. *The First Ladies Cook Book: Favorite Recipes of all the Presidents of the United States*. New York: Parents' Magazine Press, 1969.

Phillips, Louis. *Ask Me Anything About the Presidents*. Ormond Beach, Fla.: Camelot Publishing, 1992.

Rubel, David. *Encyclopedia of Presidents and Their Times*. New York: Scholastic, 1997.

Sabin, Louis. *Andrew Jackson: Frontier Patriot*. Kansas City: Troll Associates, 1986.

Sinnott, Susan. *Sarah Childress Polk: 1803-1891*. Danbury, Conn.: Children's Press, 1998.

Sullivan, George. *Facts and Fun About the Presidents*. New York: Scholastic, 1987.

Trefouse, Hans Louis. *Andrew Johnson: A Biography*. New York: W. W. Norton and Company, 1989.

Whitney, David C. *The American Presidents*. Garden City, N. Y.: Doubleday, 1969.

Williams, Frank Broyles, Jr. *Tennessee's Presidents*. Knoxville: University of Tennessee Press, 1981.

Chapter Five

TWO TO TEXAS
Why Davy Crockett and Sam Houston Wouldn't Stay in Tennessee

Davy Crockett was "half horse and half alligator, with a little touch of snapping turtle thrown in for good measure. He could run faster, jump higher, squat lower, dive deeper, stay under longer, and come out drier than any man in the whole country."

Davy Crockett, buckskin pioneer
(Courtesy TSLA)

That's how someone described one of Tennessee's most famous and colorful historical figures.

Dressed in leather breeches and moccasins, with a tomahawk stuck in his belt, a bullet pouch and powder horn slung across his shoulder, and a coonskin cap resting snugly atop his head, Davy Crockett was a genuine Tennessee "buckskin pioneer."

It's hard to know just where the truth about Davy Crockett's life ends and the tall tales begin. That's because while Crockett was living, he loved to tell exaggerated stories about himself. After he died, his legend grew and grew until he became one of the most well-known figures in American history.

Many of the legends about Davy Crockett deal with his sure-fire aim as a marksman. One story tells about a shooting match where Crockett's opponent shot dead center in the bull's-eye. The man turned to Davy and smiled smugly. "Think you can beat that?" he asked.

Crockett raised his rifle, aimed, and fired. His bullet hit smack dab on top of his opponent's, splitting it in two.

"Yep, I think so," Davy answered as he walked away.

Another story says that Davy's wife was so confident of his shooting ability that she once stood against a tree and let him shoot a comb out of her hair. Like many of the stories about Davy Crockett, no one is quite sure that the story is true.

The most famous tale of all, one Crockett himself was fond of telling, claims that late one afternoon, Davy's dog treed a fat raccoon.

As Davy lifted his gun to shoot, the raccoon threw up his hands. He said, "Hold on a minute. Ain't you Davy Crockett?"

"That's right."

"Then save your ammunition. I surrender." With that, the coon jumped into Crockett's tow sack.

Replica of the cabin where Crockett was born (Courtesy TSLA)

A lot of the things people know about Davy Crockett's life come from reading his 1834 autobiography, *A Narrative of the Life of David Crockett of the State of Tennessee.*

Davy Crockett was born in 1786 in a tiny log cabin near Limestone, Tennessee. "My ancestry was poor, but I hope honest," he said. "My father and mother had six sons and three daughters. I was the fifth son."

All the Crockett boys loved to hunt the squirrels, rabbits, wild turkeys, deer, and bears that provided meat for the family table, but none of them loved to hunt as much as Davy did. From the time he was barely old enough to walk, he practiced slinking through the woods as quietly as an Indian, trying hard not to break twigs or crunch leaves so he wouldn't scare animals away.

Davy never spent much time in school. In fact, he didn't learn to read and write until he was sixteen years old. But he made up for his lack of "book learning" with plenty of knowledge about the real world.

When he was only twelve years old, he helped a man drive a herd of cattle from East Tennessee to Virginia, covering the entire 400 miles on foot. And when he was thirteen, he ran away from home to escape his father's anger and was gone for almost three years.

Like Davy Crockett, Sam Houston was one of nine children. Born in Virginia in 1793, he moved to East Tennessee with his widowed mother and his brothers and sisters when he was fourteen years old. His brothers made a living farming and running a store near Maryville.

But Sam hated farming and storekeeping. When he was sixteen, he ran away from home and went to live with a group of Cherokee Indians on an island in the Tennessee River.

"I prefer measuring deer tracks to measuring tape," he said when people asked why he had left white civilization.

Sam loved to hunt, fish, and swim. The Cherokees helped him hone those skills. Chief John Jolly was so impressed with Sam that he adopted him and named him "The Raven." Jolly taught Sam the Cherokee language and customs. Houston often said that he owed

Sam "The Raven" Houston in Cherokee costume (Courtesy TSLA)

his bravery and leadership ability to what he learned while living with the Indians.

Though Sam never cared much for school, he loved to read. He especially enjoyed books about heroes. His favorite hero story was the ancient Greek epic *The Iliad*. He committed huge portions of the poem to memory. Sam was certain that he, like the hero in *The Iliad*, was destined for greatness.

After living with the Cherokees for three years, Sam returned to Maryville. He was in debt and believed that he could earn some money by opening a private school.

He was right. Houston's reputation as a teacher grew. People didn't care that he was young and had little formal education. They talked about his bright mind, his enthusiasm, and his love for literature. The school was soon full and so popular that Sam was able to charge a higher tuition than any other school in the area. Students who couldn't afford the eight-dollar-per-term fee in cash were allowed to pay in corn or in calico cloth.

After six months as a schoolmaster, Sam Houston had earned enough money to pay off all his debts. He closed the school and never again worked as a teacher. But later in life he said that teaching gave him "a higher self-satisfaction than any office or honor I have since held."

Davy Crockett was barely grown when he decided that he needed a wife. "So I went out to hunt me one," he wrote in his autobiography. When he first laid eyes on young Polly Finley, he knew she was the girl for him. She was "pretty to look at, interesting to talk to, and sweeter than sugar," Davy said.

Polly fell head over heels in love with Davy, too. The couple married and soon had two sons. That's when Crockett decided to move farther west in Tennessee. "I found I was better at increasing my family than my fortune," he wrote. "I thought it best to move before my family got too large, so that I might have less to carry."

In Alabama there lived a group of Creek Indians known as "Red Sticks" because they carried red war clubs. In 1813 the Red Sticks attacked a fort and murdered more than 200 people.

Crockett volunteered to help General Andrew Jackson's army troops seek vengeance. He proved his worth both as a scout and as a hunter who supplied the hungry troops with meat, but when his sixty days of volunteer duty were up, he returned home to Polly.

———

Sam Houston also volunteered to fight the Creek Indians. Before he left for Alabama to join General Jackson's Tennessee troops, his mother told him this: "While the door to my cabin is open to brave men, it is eternally shut against cowards."

Then she gave him a ring. On it was engraved the word *Honor*.

During the Battle of Horseshoe Bend against the Red Sticks in March 1814, Sam showed that he had taken his mother's words to heart. While leading a group of soldiers over a wall, he was shot in the thigh by a barbed arrow. Though he tried to remove it himself, he could not.

He called to his lieutenant. "Pull this arrow from my leg," he ordered. Though the man pulled with all his strength, he could not dislodge the arrow.

"Sir, it's buried too deep in your muscle," he told Houston. "These arrowheads are designed to do more damage coming out of a man than going in. I simply can't get it loose."

"Keep trying," Houston replied.

The man pulled harder on the arrow, but it would not budge. He shook his head in dismay. "I can't. . . ."

With that, Houston raised his sword high over his head. "Try again," he said. "And if you fail this time, I will smite you to the earth!"

With all his might, the man yanked at the arrow. It finally came loose, along with a great deal of Sam Houston's blood and flesh. When General Jackson rode by and saw how badly Houston was wounded, he ordered him not to return to battle.

But just a short while later, Sam heard his comrades' cries for help. He charged into the thick of the fighting and immediately received two Indian bullets in his right shoulder. He collapsed onto the ground in pain and exhaustion.

Though Jackson's troops eventually defeated the Creeks, they feared it had been at the price of Sam Houston's life. Doctors gave him no hope of survival and left him on the battlefield with the other dying men.

But Sam Houston was too tough to die. More than a year after he had left his mother's home, he finally returned to her—pale, gaunt, and battle scarred, but alive. The ring she had given him was still on his finger. He wore it for the rest of his life.

After recovering from his war wounds, Sam Houston decided to study law. He passed the bar exam and, at the age of twenty-five, set up a law practice in Lebanon, Tennessee. He was soon elected district attorney and in 1821 became commander of the Tennessee state militia.

Just a few months after Davy Crockett returned home from the Creek War, tragedy struck. "Death entered my humble cottage and tore from my children an affectionate good mother, and from me a tender and loving wife," Davy wrote. Polly Crockett was only twenty-seven years old when she died.

Davy was left alone to care for his two boys and an infant daughter. "I soon realized that I must have another wife," he recalled. "There lived in the neighborhood a widow lady, Elizabeth Patton, with two children of her own. We soon bargained, and got married."

The Crockett family grew to include four more children. They often piled into a wagon and moved to a different spot in Tennessee, one where Davy would build a new log cabin and hope to make a more prosperous living. He tried his hand at farming and milling and making wooden barrels, but met with little success at any of those occupations.

The one thing he was good at, other than hunting, was telling stories. That's what eventually made Davy Crockett a success in politics.

He was elected justice of the peace and town commissioner of Lawrenceburg, Tennessee, before setting his mind on a bigger prize—the state legislature.

Davy quickly learned that many voters were more interested in hearing entertaining stories than in listening to serious political debates.

After his opponents had droned on and on about government issues, Davy would stand up and tell about the bear cub one of his daughters had brought home in her pocket.

"We tamed that cub and named him 'Death Hug,'" Davy would joke to his appreciative audience. "He sits at the table with the Crockett family now and eats like a man. Sometimes he reads to us, if he can find his glasses."

Then he'd tell about the thirty-seven-foot-long alligator he'd lassoed and made into a pet. "He lays in the yard beside our cabin in the summertime. We use him as a bench." The crowd would roar with laughter.

In 1821 Crockett was elected to the Tennessee House of Representatives. A few of the more sophisticated lawmakers thought Crockett was an ignorant country bumpkin.

Some legislators wore fine suits and fancy ruffled shirts, and they looked down their noses at Davy's coonskin cap and deerskin clothing. One legislator, referring to the fact that Crockett was from a rough and unsettled part of the state, mockingly referred to him as "the gentleman from the cane."

Crockett didn't have a hot temper, but he didn't like for people to make fun of him, either. He bought a set of fine white ruffles. The next day, when he rose to speak in the legislature, the ruffles were pinned to his buckskin coat. Many of the lawmakers laughed and clapped. Davy had won their respect with his humor.

Davy Crockett served two terms in the state legislature. Then some of his friends urged him to seek a seat in Congress. He agreed, and in 1825 he ran for the U.S. House of Representatives. He lost, but by only two votes. And he learned some important lessons about politics.

He kept telling funny stories instead of talking about issues, just as he'd done when campaigning for the state legislature. When one of his opponents made the same long, boring speech every time a crowd gathered, Davy decided to play a trick on him. He memorized the speech.

Then one day when Davy was chosen to speak first, he delivered that speech word for word. His opponent was so flustered that he couldn't even reply.

Crockett also learned the value of giving small presents to potential voters. "In one pocket of my buckskin shirt, I'd carry a bottle of whisky," he wrote. "In the other I'd have a plug of chewing tobacco. That way, when a fellow had spit his own tobacco out to have a drink, I could replace it with a fresh chaw."

His tactics worked. Beginning in 1827, he was elected to Congress three times.

Four years earlier, in 1823, Sam Houston had run unopposed for a seat in the U.S. Congress. He was elected again in 1825. He spent most of his time in Washington promoting the interests of his friend and fellow Tennessean Andrew Jackson.

Sam returned to Tennessee in 1827 to run for governor. Like Davy Crockett, Houston was a gifted campaigner. He traveled around the state on a majestic gray stallion and stopped to talk wherever a crowd gathered.

It was hard not to notice Sam Houston. He was a tall man—Tennesseans claimed he was six feet, two inches tall, but Texans later insisted he was closer to six feet, six inches. Dressed in fancy breeches and a ruffled shirt, with a beaver hat atop his head and a red beaded Indian sash thrown across his shoulder, he was a handsome, dashing figure.

When Sam Houston talked, people listened. And they elected him governor of Tennessee.

Houston wanted a wife. Eighteen-year-old Eliza Allen seemed to

SAM HOUSTON AT THIRTY-THREE.
Military hero, Congressman, protége of Andrew Jackson
and Tennessee's young Man of Destiny.
(A miniature on ivory painted by J. Wood in Washington,
1826. The earliest known authentic likeness of Houston.
At various times in the possession of Houston's sister,
Eliza Moore, Eliza Allen, General Jackson, and Mrs.
Robert McEwen, of Nashville. Reproduced by courtesy
of General Houston's granddaughter, Mrs. Robert A. John,
of Houston)

Sam Houston at age 33
(Courtesy TSLA)

be perfect for the job. She was a beautiful, high-spirited girl from a well-to-do Nashville family. And her parents were eager for her to marry the governor.

But Eliza was not at all eager to be Tennessee's First Lady if it meant marrying Sam Houston. For one thing, he was thirty-five years old—practically old enough to be her father. For another, she disliked politics. But Sam and her family kept after her for so long that she finally said yes.

The marriage was doomed from the start. It was obvious that Eliza didn't love Sam—it was even whispered that she was in love with someone else. Sam Houston was a heavy drinker, and Eliza hated that. Some people who were close to her said that she found the scars from the wounds Sam had received during the Creek War so repulsive that she couldn't bear to look at him in his nightclothes.

Whatever the reason, Eliza left Sam after only a few short months of marriage. Although he begged her to come back, she refused.

Sam Houston was too humiliated to continue as governor. He resigned, packed his bags, and headed west.

<hr>

While Davy Crockett was in Congress, one of the issues that concerned him the most was making it easier for poor people to buy land. Another was the right of American Indians to live where they wanted. That issue caused him to butt heads with the President of the United States—Tennessee's own Andrew Jackson.

Jackson wanted to force Indian tribes who lived in the southeastern United States to move to territory west of the Mississippi River. Every member of Congress from Tennessee agreed with him, except Davy Crockett.

"My conscience demands I stand for the right, even if it pits me against the President," Crockett said. "I refuse to force these once powerful people to give up what is rightfully theirs."

Several of his colleagues warned that he would ruin his political career by opposing Andrew Jackson.

Davy Crockett the lawmaker
(Courtesy TSLA)

But Crockett remained firm. "The Indian Removal Act is a wicked, unjust measure. I will go against it."

Sure enough, Davy Crockett was defeated in 1835 when he ran for reelection. He had made a promise before the voting took place. "If I lose, I will leave the country and go to Texas."

And that's just what he did.

Sam Houston left the country, too, after his marriage failed. He went to stay with his old friend John Jolly and the Cherokee people who lived in the Arkansas Territory west of the Mississippi River.

Sam wore Indian clothes and spoke the Cherokee language. He let his hair and beard grow long. He set up a trading post and worked hard to promote peace among various Indian tribes. He wrote editorials on their behalf for an Arkansas newspaper. The

Sam Houston on horseback (Courtesy TSLA)

Cherokees were so grateful that they made him an honorary citizen.

But that was not enough to make Sam Houston happy. More and more often, he tried to drown his sorrows in whisky. Soon the Cherokees had a new name for him. They didn't call him The Raven anymore. They called him "The Big Drunk."

Although he was not legally divorced from Eliza, in 1829 Sam married a Cherokee woman named Tiana Rogers. Their union was a happy one, though Houston was often gone from home. He made a trip to Nashville to visit his mother just before she died. Then he traveled to Washington, D.C., to speak to Congress in behalf of Indian rights.

When he finally returned to Cherokee country in 1832, he said good-bye to Tiana forever. He gave her his house, his land, and other property they had shared.

Then he climbed onto his horse and headed for Texas.

In those days Texas was part of Mexico, but more and more Americans were moving there all the time. Those Americans believed that Texas ought to belong to the United States. They formed an army to fight the Mexicans and chose Sam Houston as their leader.

In San Antonio, Texas, is an old Spanish mission called the Alamo. Early in 1836, some American soldiers turned the Alamo into a fort. Colonel Jim Bowie and Colonel William Travis were in charge of the 150 men holed up there.

When Davy Crockett heard they needed help, he gathered a group of Tennesseans together to help defend the Alamo against the Mexicans. "I have come to aid you in your noble cause," he told them when he arrived at the fort.

In late February, the Mexicans laid siege to the Alamo. They fired their cannons and shot their guns at the men inside. For almost two weeks the Americans remained unharmed, but their food and ammunition supplies were running low.

Davy Crockett did his best to keep the men entertained with his quick wit and good humor. He played the fiddle and performed songs and dances from his childhood. He told tall tales and made encouraging speeches.

"I just know my old friend Sam Houston will pull us out of this mess," he told his companions. "Any day now he'll send more soldiers and supplies."

The Alamo (Courtesy TSLA)

Several weeks earlier, Sam Houston had warned the men at the Alamo to leave. "The Texas Army isn't big or strong enough yet to beat the Mexicans," he told them. "Get out before it's too late!"

But his orders were ignored. Travis, Bowie, and Crockett were confident that they could defeat the Mexican Army.

Just before dawn on March 6, a cry went up from one of the American sentinels inside the Alamo. "The Mexicans are coming!" The men sprang to their posts. "Victory or death!" they shouted as they began firing at the enemy.

Within minutes, nearly 2,000 Mexican troops overran the Alamo. They used battering rams—huge logs carried by several men—to knock down the gates. They climbed over the walls with scaling ladders. With guns blazing and bayonets flashing, the battle raged inside the walls of the fort.

In the end, there were too many Mexicans and not enough Texans. By sunup, all the American soldiers, including Davy Crockett, lay dead.

For several weeks after the Alamo fell, Sam Houston refused to allow his men to fight the Mexicans. The soldiers complained. It looked to them like Houston was running away, and they couldn't understand why. But Houston had a plan.

He lured the Mexican army onto a marsh near the San Jacinto River. He ordered his men to burn the bridge that would allow the Mexicans to retreat. Then he waited.

On the afternoon of April 21, 1836, the Mexican soldiers were taking a siesta. Houston knew that the time was right to attack.

"Remember the Alamo!" he yelled as he charged into battle.

"Remember the Alamo!" his soldiers yelled as they followed him.

In less than twenty minutes, the fighting was finished. Hundreds of Mexicans lay dead. The rest, including their leader, General Santa Anna, were taken prisoner. Santa Anna agreed to grant Texas independence from Mexico.

Sam Houston was soon the most popular man in Texas—The Hero of San Jacinto.

Santa Anna surrenders to Houston. (Courtesy TSLA)

Though Davy Crockett was dead, his legend lived on. A play called *The Lion of the West*, based on Crockett's life, had been popular in Washington, D.C., while he was a Congressman. Several years later, another theatrical production based on Davy's favorite saying, *"Be Sure You're Right, Then Go Ahead,"* delighted audiences in the United States and England.

The silent motion picture *Davy Crockett* was a hit in 1916. And in 1960 John Wayne starred as the famous Tennessee frontiersman in the movie *The Alamo*.

But it was Walt Disney who guaranteed that Davy's fame would last forever. In the mid 1950s, his Davy Crockett movies and television series started a "Crockett craze" among children in the United States.

Stores set up special Davy Crockett departments to sell records, lunch boxes, towels, wallets, baby shoes, school supplies, dishes, and (of course) fringed deerskin coats and coonskin caps. Those caps became so popular that the price of coonskins rose from twenty-five cents to six dollars a pound in the 1950s!

More than 100 years after his death, Davy Crockett—the King of the Wild Frontier—lives on in the hearts of the American people.

Sam Houston went on to become another Tennessean-turned-Texan whose flamboyant personality fascinated the American public. Soon after his victory at San Jacinto, he was elected President of the newly formed Republic of Texas. After Texas became a state in 1846, he was elected U.S. Senator, and later became governor—the only man ever to have served as governor of two different states.

Texas President Sam Houston
(Courtesy TSLA)

BIBLIOGRAPHY

Allen, Michael. "Who Was David Crockett?" *Tennessee: State of the Nation*. Boston: American Heritage, 1998.

Crawford, Ann Fears. *Sam Houston: American Hero*. Dallas: Hendrick-Long, 1993.

Crockett, David. *A Narrative of the Life of David Crockett of the State of Tennessee*. Philadelphia: Carey, Hart, and Company, 1834.

Fritz, Jean. *Make Way for Sam Houston*. New York: G. P. Putnam's Sons, 1986.

Kanon, Thomas. "The Battle of Horseshoe Bend." *Tennessee Historical Quarterly*, Spring 1999.

Mosley, Elizabeth R. *Davy Crockett: Hero of the Wild Frontier*. Broomall, Penn.: Chelsea House Publishers, 1991.

Parks, Aileen Wells. *Davy Crockett: Young Rifleman*. New York: Aladdin Books, 1986.

Sanford, William R. and Carl R. Green. *Sam Houston: Texas Hero*. Berkeley Heights, N. J.: Enslow Publishers, 1996.

Turner, Martha Ann. S*am Houston and His Twelve Women: The Ladies Who Influenced the Life of Texas' Greatest Statesman*. Austin: Pemberton Press, 1966.

Zorn, Steven. *Classic American Folk Tales*. Philadelphia: Courage Books, 1992.

Chapter Six

BROTHER AGAINST BROTHER
Whose Side Are We on in This War?

Try to imagine living in a nation split apart by war. A nation where people who once called themselves "Americans" instead became "Yankees" or "Rebels." A nation where men with a common heritage put on uniforms of different colors and killed more than half a million of their own countrymen.

My name is Amanda McDowell. I lived through such a time.

The Civil War didn't just divide my country. It divided my home state of Tennessee. And it divided the community where I lived—White County, a part of the mountainous Upper Cumberland region of Middle Tennessee.

Worst of all, the war divided the McDowell family. My two brothers fought on opposite sides—Lafayette as a soldier in the Confederate Army, Jackson as a courier for the Union Army.

Our family owned a boarding school called Cumberland Institute, built on a hilltop in the Cherry Creek community near Sparta. Our widowed father, Curtis McDowell, served as headmaster and teacher. My sister, Mary, and I taught classes and helped in every other way we could.

I was a young woman barely out of my teens when the war began. During those years I kept a diary. I tried to write in it often, believing that someday people might like to read about what life was like for a family like mine during that horrible war. I also kept all the letters my brothers sent us.

In June 1861, Tennessee became the eleventh and final state to secede from the Union and join the Confederate States of America. In my diary I wrote:

I guess Tennessee is voted out of the Union. I do not believe it would have been if people had been allowed to vote their true sentiments. Nearly all the Union men in this neighborhood stayed home, not wishing to get into a brawl and deeming it a hopeless cause. Oh what a fair country and what a glorious government have the politicians ruined! I consider the whole business to be wrong! Fayette talks of volunteering. I should hate to see him start to war, for I do not think it is right to fight against the government.

Lafayette, whom we called "Fayette," had been teaching school in a nearby town. He wrote a letter to us in April 1861:

The war fever is very high in these parts. I think a bloody war is inevitable. I wish to join the Confederate cavalry. I intend to volunteer as soon as I see where my services ought to be rendered. I shall not be satisfied until I give aid to my countrymen.

My other brother, Jackson, whom we called "Jack," was the editor of a weekly newspaper, the *Cookeville Times*, in a town about eight miles north of where we lived. Jack did not share Fayette's opinion about the war. Although he loved Tennessee, he believed that joining the Confederacy was wrong. He was not hesitant about expressing his opinions on the editorial pages of his newspaper:

There is a better way to settle differences than going to war. . . . It is a mistake for Southerners to destroy the country and themselves. . . . Slavery is as bad for slave owners as it is for slaves; it damages all who practice it. . . . Secession is wrong. . . . Discussion is better than bloodshed.

Some of the people who read Jack's newspaper agreed with him, but many did not. Even though few people in the Upper Cumberland owned slaves, many of them believed the federal government had no right to abolish slavery. Some of Jack's friends warned him to stop printing anti-Confederate opinions.

In a letter to our father, Fayette wrote:

Persuade Jack to quit printing Union sentiments or anything else. He can do no good and is doing much harm.

Jackson McDowell
(Courtesy Betty McDowell)

Father did his best to avoid taking sides, but he feared that the war would close our school and shatter our community. "There will be ill will and hatred among people who were friends that will not die out even in your lifetime," he warned the students. "You are the ones who will suffer on the battlefield. I will suffer here."

Even after Tennessee voted to secede, Father kept the American flag flying over Cumberland Institute. It was a special flag—one that Mary and I had sewn ourselves several years earlier. One evening a group of men, their hats pulled low and their faces covered with handkerchiefs so that we would not recognize them, rode onto our property.

"Where is the schoolmaster?" they demanded.

"He's not available right now," I answered softly, hoping that my voice would not reveal the fear in my heart.

With that, the men tore the flag from its pole and threw it to the ground. Then they began stomping on it until it was torn to pieces. "Tell Mr. McDowell that's what we think of his flag!" one of them shouted as they galloped away.

Mary and I gathered up the pieces and washed them. Later, we made two quilts from the remains of that flag—a red and white one for her and a blue and white one for me. We hoped those quilts would always remain in our family.

When Fayette learned what had happened, he asked if we would like to have a Confederate flag to fly over the school. "It might keep you safe from bushwhackers," he told us.

"No," we answered. "Flying the Rebel flag might offend Jack. We won't do it."

We were true to our word. For the remainder of the war, no flag

Blue quilt sewn from torn American flag
(Courtesy Bets Ramsey and Merikay Waldvogel.
Photo by Gary Heatherly in *Southern Quilts: Surviving Relics of the Civil War*. Nashville, Tenn.: Rutledge Hill Press, 1998.)

flew over our beloved Cumberland Institute.

Bushwhackers were lawless men who roamed the countryside during the war. They were not real soldiers—most of them were too cowardly to join the army. They spent their time stealing livestock and food and destroying property. Sometimes they murdered innocent people.

The most famous Confederate bushwhacker in our part of the state was Champ Ferguson. He and his followers terrorized the citizens of White County throughout the war, often abusing or killing anyone who tried to resist them. They used *guerrilla warfare*—sneaking up on their enemies, whether Union troops or Tennessee civilians, and opening fire. Ferguson and his men had no shame. Once, they attacked a group of people attending a church service, killing one person and injuring two.

And the bushwhackers on the Union side were just as bad. Their leader was Tinker Dave Beatty—a man who seemed to have no conscience at all. Beatty and his gang destroyed and killed for what sometimes seemed to be pure meanness.

After Fayette joined the army, he was assigned to a Confederate company stationed not far from our home. We were always fearful of what might happen to him, as I told my diary in the summer of 1861:

> I do not know whether Fayette will ever come home or not. I believe this will be an unjust and unholy war and I am loathe to see him engage in it. . . . If I thought he would come back as dissipated as some of the soldiers, I would

rather he would go to his grave. . . . His food is beef, bacon, and flour bread with no way to cook it. They have a camp kettle and frying pan and no dish at all, not even a dish rag or a bit of soap. . . . I worked all day sewing him a pair of pants which he may have to be buried in for all I know.

Tennessee was directly in the path of the Union Army as it drove into the Deep South. More Civil War battles were fought in our state than anyplace else. Fort Henry and Fort Donelson, Shiloh, Franklin, Nashville—the list goes on and on. These were my thoughts after one of the battles:

> There are many widows and orphans who were not so just weeks ago. . . . If the makers of this war had some of the evils to bear, they would be a little more willing to stop it. . . . There are so many rumors afloat that we hardly believe anything we hear. . . . I do not know what kind of principle men can have who will wage the continuance of so dreadful a thing as this war.

For many months after the war started, Jack resisted joining either the Union or Confederate army. He believed that words were more powerful than guns and hoped his newspaper columns might persuade readers that the war was madness.

"I am bound to stand for the government," he said soon after the war began, "but a man is hardly allowed to express his opinion now unless he is for the South."

Those words were soon to prove truer than Jack could have realized. In early spring of 1862, a drunken mob led by Champ Ferguson stormed his newspaper office. Their plan was to destroy the printing press and then to hang Jack for his Union sentiments.

Luckily, Jack escaped before the mob could capture him. He decided that the best thing to do was flee to Kentucky, but first he wished to come home to see Father, Mary, and me again—perhaps for the last time. Fearing discovery at our cabin, Jack hid in a nearby cave. As we visited with him, Mary could not control her tongue.

"Jack, I wish you would join the Confederates and go with Fayette. I would feel so much better if the two of you were together."

Jack shook his head sadly. "No, Mary. If I fight, I will fight against Fayette's side, though I pray for his safety always. I am against secession and slavery. I will not oppose my country—the United States of America. I must go far away and live among strangers. That way, if I do have to kill, I won't be forced to kill my neighbors and perhaps even my own brother."

Mary's eyes filled with tears, as did Father's and mine. Then Jack made a promise. "If I live, I will come back here, win or lose!" He handed Father a bag filled with money and disappeared into the night. We could do nothing but watch him go.

Meanwhile, Fayette continued his duties with the Confederate Army. During the early months of the war, he (like many of the Confederate sympathizers) believed that the South was headed for an easy victory. His letters to us were filled with hope:

> It is astonishing to see the enthusiasm of our soldiers. I am satisfied by seeing the cowardice of the Yankees and mad bravery of the Southerners that the South is bound to conquer. . . . The officers are in good spirits, fully believing the North will quit us before long.

But as the war dragged on month after month, hopes for a quick end to the fighting grew dim. Very few students remained at our school. Some had returned to their homes to farm and look after their families. Many of the young men had gone to war. My diary in June 1862 read:

> Some of our former students march after the drum, with a sword or musket in the ranks of the Confederate Army under a new flag. . . . Others march under the glorious old Stars and Stripes, and they who were once united in the strongest bonds of friendship are now ready to kill each other. . . . God pity the poor soldiers, and forgive those who have caused all this.

We learned that Jack had been captured and thrown in jail while on his way to Kentucky. He was accused of stealing, a crime of which we all knew he was innocent. His only real "crime" had been speaking out for what he thought was right.

Jack eventually escaped and joined a Union Army company near Knoxville. Insisting that he supported their cause, he pleaded that they not force him to become a soldier.

"I cannot fight in an area where I might have to kill my friends or my brother," he told the commanding officer.

"Then we will see what other job we can assign to you," the man replied.

The officer soon discovered that Jack had many valuable skills. He could figure how much food the soldiers needed and then bargain with nearby farmers to purchase it. My brother was unmatched as a marksman, although he insisted that he wished to shoot only game, not people. And Jack was an accomplished rider, even on the most poorly trained horses.

When the officer discovered that Jack had a photographic memory, he knew what job to give him. Jackson McDowell would become a courier for the Union Army.

Jack had no need to write notes on paper—he could memorize whatever was required of him. He carried information about battle plans and other news to scattered army camps, first in Tennessee, then throughout several other states. For two years he rode about the country delivering important messages to Union troops, reciting what he had memorized word for word.

Jack never officially enlisted in the Army, though he was paid a lieutenant's wage for his work. He never wore a uniform.

And in all that time, we never heard one word from him, nor he from us.

Fayette was in poor health. He had been given an impure vaccination when he enlisted in the Confederate Army and had never fully regained his strength. He often wrote home telling of the wretched conditions under which he lived:

> I am tired of the war. I hope it will end soon. . . . We lived ten days on cold bread and beef without shelter. I wish those in favor of carrying on this war had to eat a whole cow, hoofs and all, every day one each. I mean, until they are ready to quit.

Fayette sent us money whenever he could, though the Confederate dollars he was paid were nearly as worthless as the paper they were printed on. It didn't matter much though, since there was very little to buy even if we'd had good money.

Mary and I busied ourselves with never-ending chores—tending the garden and animals, cooking, and doing laundry.

And sewing—that was the job we never seemed to finish. There was no cloth of any kind to be purchased, so every item we made came completely from scratch. We clipped the wool from the sheep, washed it, carded it, spun the thread, and dyed the thread. Then we wove the cloth, cut, tailored, and sewed every piece of clothing we made.

It seemed that no sooner were we finished than we'd receive another letter from Fayette requesting a new gray coat or a pair of trousers.

Soldiers from both armies often passed through our little community. Fayette warned us about them in his letters:

> Don't worry about the Yanks wanting the tools or the furniture. If you had a horse or a sow they would pay you a visit, though. . . . Keep on hand plenty to eat and nothing more, for our own soldiers are as apt to find your house and take your supplies as the Yankees.

In my diary I wrote:

> The Rebels are gone and the Yanks are in. (I wonder what makes us say Yankees. There are very few Yankees among them.) They take it time about, and one does about as much good as the other. And we could do very well without either.

Though we never went hungry, some of our neighbors did. Prices for basic necessities were out of reach. Flour sold for $250 a barrel and black-eyed peas for forty-five dollars a bushel. No one could afford twelve dollars a pound for coffee, so we made our own from parched oats, with sorghum molasses for sweetener. Because salt could not be purchased, many folks dug up the dirt floors of their smokehouses and boiled the salt out to use again.

As the war years dragged on and conditions worsened in every way, I wrote:

> The country is hard up for food and livestock. . . . Many a family has been left without corn for bread, or a hog, or a cow. The soldiers—Confederate and Yankee—take anything they want without paying for it but I can scarcely blame

them. They are so cold and hungry. By the time this war is over, the South will have been milked dry. I fear the years to follow will be hard ones.

Due to his poor health, Fayette left the Confederate Army in 1864 and came home. We were overjoyed, of course. In early 1865, we received wonderful news. Jack was alive and living in Kentucky. He was working as a lawyer and owned a profitable sawmill. Because of his Union sympathies, he was afraid to return to Tennessee. He wrote to us:

I have quit everything like politics and become mute upon all political questions, but I am ever a Union man and for Lincoln for the Presidency. Father, give up everything you have and bring the family here to Kentucky immediately. All you have to do is get to Scott County, Tennessee, and I will meet you there. You can walk that far.

Though we were thankful that Jack was alive and well, Father did not want to leave his beloved Cumberland Institute. Our enrollment was increasing as crippled soldiers, maimed and demoralized by the war but hungry for an education, returned to school. And so we stayed put in White County.

Four long and horrible years after it had begun, the Civil War finally came to an end. In the spring of 1865 I wrote:

General Robert E. Lee and his whole Confederate Army is taken. Truly secession has been the greatest tyrant that ever ruled over this country. I do rejoice at the prospect of peace. . . . The news of President Lincoln's death is confirmed. There are plenty here who are glad of it, but they may have to regret it. . . . I guess the peace is made. That is all I care much for. The soldiers have all come that are alive and able to get here. They say they are not whipped but "overpowered" but I wonder what is the difference.

Predictions that the South would continue to suffer even after the war ended came true. White County—sometimes described as a no-man's-land—was a long time in regaining its former strength and prosperity.

McDowell family graves, Cherry Creek
Cemetery, White County
(Photo by Karl Klein)

Jackson McDowell grave, Mt. Pisgah
Cemetery, White County
(Photo by Karl Klein)

A great number of the stores, factories, churches, and schools that had shut down during the war never reopened. Many people moved away. But my family—the McDowells—stayed.

And we prospered. Jack kept his promise and returned home after the war ended. He and Fayette went into business together and did quite well. All of us married and had children, which made our father a very happy grandpa who lived to be eighty years old. Sadly, Fayette never recovered from the illnesses brought on from soldiering. He died when he was but forty years of age.

The rest of us have carried on, forever changed by our experiences during the terrible four years that split our nation apart, but proud to be Tennesseans—and Americans.

BIBLIOGRAPHY

Blankenship, Lela McDowell. *Fiddles in the Cumberlands*. New York: Richard R. Smith Company, 1943.

Blankenship, Lela McDowell. *When Yesterday Was Today*. Nashville: Tennessee Book Company, 1966.

Dudney, Betty Jane. "Civil War in White County, Tennessee, 1861-1865." M. A. Thesis, Tennessee Technological University, 1985.

Ramsey, Bets and Merikay Waldvogel. *Southern Quilts: Surviving Relics of the Civil War*. Nashville: Rutledge Hill Press, 1998.

Chapter Seven

DRINK COCA-COLA IN BOTTLES!

A Chattanoogan Has a Refreshing Idea

Coca-Cola. Just the name brings to mind visions of ice-cold cans or frosty bottles of the world's favorite soft drink.

But it hasn't always been that way. For the first few years after Coca-Cola was invented, it was served only in a glass. A couple of Tennesseans trying to get rich came up with the idea of putting Coca-Cola in containers that people could take with them.

Coca-Cola was invented in Atlanta, Georgia, in 1886 by a pharmacist named John Pemberton. Pemberton liked to experiment with making and selling different kinds of medicines. One of his most popular products was a syrup called "Coca-Cola."

One of the ingredients in Coca-cola was caffeine. To cover up its bitter taste, Pemberton added lots of sugar to his syrup. He also. put in citric acid and fruit flavors to make it taste better.

Pemberton mixed the syrup in a huge kettle hung over a fire in his backyard. He funneled it through sand filters into pint-sized bottles. Then he sold it to drugstores as a "brain and nerve tonic" which could cure headaches, upset stomachs, and other nervous illnesses.

Instructions on every bottle told customers to mix the syrup with water before drinking it.

In 1888 another Atlanta pharmacist named Asa Candler bought the rights to Coca-Cola from Pemberton. Candler had one of the largest drugstore businesses in Atlanta. He sold the syrup in all his stores and persuaded other pharmacists to buy it.

How did the Coca-Cola syrup come to be a soft drink instead of a medicine? The answer to that question isn't entirely clear.

According to one legend, on a hot summer day near the turn of the twentieth century, a customer came into an Atlanta drugstore, complaining of a headache. "I need a bottle of Coca-Cola syrup right away," the man said to the store clerk. "And please get me a glass of water to mix with it, too."

Asa Candler
(Courtesy The Coca-Cola Company)

In those days, many soda fountains sold carbonated fruit drinks during the hot summer months. "How would you like to try mixing the syrup with some cold carbonated soda water instead of tap water?" the clerk asked the man.

The man shrugged. "Okay—just be quick about it. My head is throbbing!"

So the clerk mixed the Coca-Cola syrup with chilled carbonated water.

"Hey, this is delicious!" the customer remarked after gulping down the sweet, fizzy concoction. Coca-Cola the soft drink was born.

Other accounts say that the discovery of Coca-Cola as a soda fountain drink was not an accident at all. Those stories claim that John Pemberton intended Coca-Cola to be a syrup for fountain drinks, as well as a medicine, from the very beginning.

Wherever the real truth lies, one thing is certain. Word about the delightful new drink spread quickly, and Coca-Cola was soon sold at soda fountains not only in Atlanta but in many other places as well.

One place where Coke was enormously popular was Georgia's neighbor to the north—Tennessee. The popularity of the Coca-Cola fountain drink gave Chattanoogan Benjamin Franklin Thomas an idea—an idea that would forever change the way people drink soda pop.

Benjamin Franklin Thomas
(Courtesy The Coca-Cola Company)

Thomas had been stationed in Cuba in 1898 following the Spanish-American War. A bottled carbonated fruit drink called "champagne cola" was selling well there.

Why not try the same thing back home? Thomas thought to himself. Wouldn't people be eager to buy a drink in a container they could take with them instead of having to sit at a table or counter to finish it? And wouldn't Coca-Cola be the perfect drink to bottle?

Thomas's head was full of good ideas, but his pockets were not full of money. He needed a business partner. He found one in his friend and fellow attorney Joseph Brown Whitehead.

As luck would have it, another of their friends was Asa Candler's cousin, who agreed to travel from Chattanooga to Atlanta to introduce them to the owner of Coca-Cola. The men met on a hot July day in 1899.

"Mr. Candler," Thomas said, "we're here to talk to you about putting your famous soft drink in bottles."

"I believe some folks in other parts of the country are trying that already," Candler replied. "But I have no interest in becoming involved in such an enterprise."

"Yes, but—"

Candler held up both his hands before Thomas could finish his sentence. "Mr. Thomas, Mr. Whitehead," he said. "You must understand something. My business is already highly successful. I have neither the time nor the money to pursue any venture beyond selling Coca-Cola as a fountain drink."

"We wish you would at least consider our proposal," Thomas said. "It is our hope that you will allow us to bottle Coca-Cola legally, and with your blessing."

"I'll be honest with you, gentlemen," Candler replied. "Even though your idea has merit, I am reluctant to allow outsiders to bottle my drink."

"Why?"

"Because there are too many irresponsible folks who care nothing about the reputation of what they produce. I have worked hard to make my product as good as it can be. I'm afraid that allowing outsiders an official hand in my business might injure the name of Coca-Cola."

"I think you'll find, sir," Whitehead replied, "that such is not the case with Mr. Thomas and myself. We promise that if you'll allow us to

Joseph Brown Whitehead
(Courtesy The Coca-Cola Company)

bottle Coca-Cola, we will work hard to make the name better every day."

For the first time that day, Asa Candler smiled. "Very well, gentlemen," he said. "You have at least convinced me not to say 'no' right now. Give me some time to consider your proposal."

Candler spent the next several days finding out all he could about Ben Thomas and Joe Whitehead. He contacted people who knew their backgrounds and personalities. When he was satisfied that they were the kind of men who would protect the Coca-Cola name, he agreed to grant them bottling rights.

On July 21, 1899, the Coca-Cola bottling industry was officially born when Asa Candler signed a contract granting Ben Thomas and Joe Whitehead the rights to bottle Coca-Cola in most of the United States.

Legend says that Thomas and Whitehead agreed to pay one dollar for their bottling rights and that Candler never collected the dollar. No one is sure whether that story is really true.

After the contract was signed, the real work began. Thomas and Whitehead realized that they did not have enough money to start a bottling plant. They would need another partner. They asked Chattanooga businessman John Lupton to join them.

The three men pooled their money and their efforts. In September 1899, the first official Coca-Cola bottling plant opened on Market Square in Chattanooga.

In those days, most steps in the bottling process were done by hand. First, glass bottles had to be individually washed and rinsed. It was hard to clean sticky residue out of the narrow-necked bottles. Sometimes metal shot was shaken inside the bottle to loosen the sediment to try to get the bottles cleaner.

After the bottles were thoroughly washed, it was time to fill them with Coca-Cola. A pulley hoisted a ten-gallon barrel of syrup several feet off the ground. The syrup flowed down a rubber hose into the bottles. Then carbonated water was added. Next, the bottles were sealed, one at a time, using a foot-operated machine.

Sometimes accidents happened. A hose might burst and drench workers with sticky syrup. Or a pulley might break and cause a whole barrel of syrup to spill. Bottlers wore protective masks and clothing because bottles often exploded.

The first Coca-Cola bottles were sealed with *Hutchinson stoppers*. These stoppers were made of rubber and were pulled into place with a wire loop to seal the mouth of the bottle. To open the Coca-Cola, the stopper was pushed down into the bottle rather than being pulled out. When it was pushed in, it made a loud popping noise. That's how soft drinks got the nickname "pop."

The Hutchinson seal had lots of problems. It was easy to hit the wire loop accidentally and cause the bottle to spill.When the fizzy Coke touched the rubber stopper, it sometimes caused the drink to not taste like it should. Worst of all, it soon became obvious that it was unsanitary to push an unclean stopper into something a person was about to drink.

The *crimped crown* bottle cap, the same style cap used today to seal glass drink bottles, had been invented in 1892. Some drink bottlers were reluctant to change over to the new caps because it meant having to buy expensive new machinery.

But it was clear that the crown seal was a far better design than the Hutchinson stopper. By the beginning of the twentieth century, almost all drink bottlers, including those who bottled Coca-Cola, were using the crown seal.

Horse-drawn wagons distributed bottles of Coke throughout Chattanooga. "Coca-Cola! Get your ice-cold Coca-Cola right here,"

A horse-drawn Coke wagon in Knoxville, 1913
(Courtesy The Coca-Cola Company)

the wagon drivers would bark. "Coca-Cola in bottles! Only five cents!"

Chattanoogans responded in droves. In the first year of production, more than 300 gallons of Coca-Cola were put into bottles and sold.

Thomas, Whitehead, and Lupton decided that the best way to expand their business was to *franchise*—to sell the rights to bottle Coca-Cola to other businessmen all over the country. The *parent bottler* would buy syrup from The Coca-Cola Company at a discount, mark the price up a little, and sell it to franchise bottlers.

The first Coca-Cola bottles were straight-sided and had diamond-shaped labels. Some were brown, some were clear, and some were green. Those early bottles were too similar to other soft-drink bottles to please Coca-Cola executives. They wanted a bottle that was unique.

Benjamin Thomas told his fellow bottlers, "We need a distinctive package that will help us fight substitution. . . . We need a bottle which a person will recognize as a Coca-Cola bottle even when he feels it in the dark."

In 1916 the *hobbleskirt* bottle was adopted. It was named after a popular dress style that flared at the hips and narrowed so much below the knees that it almost hobbled a woman's ability to walk. The hobbleskirt bottle eventually came to symbolize Coca-Cola and is still used today.

Asa Candler believed that the amount of Coca-Cola sold as a fountain drink would always be greater than the amount sold in bottles. He was wrong. By 1928, sales of fountain Cokes and bottled Cokes were almost even.

Original "hobbleskirt" Coca-Cola bottle (Courtesy The Coca-Cola Company)

From that time on, sales of Coca-Cola in bottles and cans have far surpassed that of the fountain drink.

Before the 1930s, most businesses that sold bottled Coca-Cola iced down the drinks in wooden or metal tubs. Thirsty customers would roll up their shirtsleeves and plunge their arms elbow-deep into the frigid water in search of the coldest Coke.

Sometimes storekeepers would cut Coca-Cola syrup barrels in half and use them as coolers. In the late 1920s, square metal boxes, painted red and bearing the Coca-Cola trademark, were sold to merchants throughout the country for icing down Cokes.

By the mid 1930s, Coke "iceboxes" were replaced by electrically refrigerated, coin-operated machines. Many of the old iceboxes and early vending machines are considered valuable antiques today.

During the war, sixty-four Coca-Cola bottling plants were built overseas, almost all of them financed by the United States government. The plants provided Coca-Cola for the military forces during wartime. When the war was over, the plants remained and continued to bottle America's favorite soft drink for much of the world.

Perhaps Coca-Cola's most famous fan is the man who lives at the North Pole. Although no one claims that Santa Claus invented Coca-Cola, some people do say that Coca-Cola invented the modern-day Santa.

Prior to the 1930s, Santa Claus had been portrayed in most art and literature as either a tall thin man dressed in blue or as an elf.

Haddon Sundblom's Santa Claus, 1953
(Courtesy The Coca-Cola Company)

An artist named Haddon Sundblom changed all that. In 1931, he came up with the idea of a fat, jolly man dressed in "Coca-Cola Red" who always received an ice-cold bottle of Coke as a reward for delivering toys on Christmas Eve. Sundblom's ads forever changed the way Americans imagined Santa Claus to look. The ads also linked Christmas and Coca-Cola together in a powerful way.

One of the biggest changes ever to take place in the soft drink industry was the invention of *one-way* containers in the 1960s.

Before then, a *bottle deposit* of a few pennies was required for every Coke or other soft drink sold. When empty bottles were returned to a store, the deposit money was refunded. Bottling companies then collected, washed, and refilled the bottles. It was estimated that during its lifetime a Coke bottle would be emptied, washed, and refilled almost forty times.

When bottlers began putting their products into *no deposit, no return* bottles and aluminum cans, customers welcomed the convenience. By the early 1970s, more than forty percent of Coca-Cola products were put into one-way containers. Nowadays, almost all of it is.

In 1899 ten cases of Coke were produced each day in Chattanooga. Today, Coca-Cola bottlers the world over are able to fill 2,300 cans a minute. No matter the time or place, somewhere in the world someone is drinking Coca-Cola from a can or a bottle. Coke has even traveled into outer space with the astronauts!

Tennesseans did not invent the world's most famous soft drink, but they made it possible for people to take Coca-Cola with them wherever they go.

"Drink Coca-Cola in Bottles!" said the ad in the November 12, 1899, *Chattanooga Times*. Customers did.

And more than 100 years later, they still do.

BIBLIOGRAPHY

"Always Chattanooga: 100 Years of Coca-Cola Bottling." Chattanooga Regional History Museum. Autumn, 1999.

Irwin, Ned L. "Bottling Gold: Chattanooga's Coca-Cola." *Tennessee Historical Quarterly 51*, no. 4 (1992): 223-37.

"It's True . . . Coca-Cola Began as a Headache Cure." *Reminisce Magazine*. 1992.

Patton, Phil. *Made in USA: The Secret History of the Things That Made America*. New York: Penguin Books, 1992.

Pendergrast, Mark. *For God, Country, and Coca-Cola: The Difinitive History of the Great American Soft Drink and the Company That Makes It*. New York: Scribner, 1993.

Chapter Eight

CANDY AND COUNTRY MUSIC

Goo Goo Clusters and the Grand Ole Opry

"Go get a Goo Goo. It's . . . good."

Anyone who has ever listened to the Grand Ole Opry has probably heard that commercial for Tennessee's most famous candy bar. But lots of folks don't know what Goo Goos are, or how they came to be.

Goo Goos were invented in Nashville in 1903 by Howell Campbell, owner of the Standard Candy Company. Campbell's company had about a dozen employees and two giant copper kettles. Standard Candy Company produced several different types of sweets, including suckers, marshmallows, and fine chocolates.

But it was a sweet treat made of caramel, marshmallows, roasted peanuts, and milk chocolate that made the company famous.

The Goo Goo Cluster was the world's first "combination" candy bar. It looked different from most candy bars, too, because it was formed into a lumpy circular cluster rather than a smooth rectangle or square.

The gooey confection was so hard to wrap that at first it was sold from under a glass counter like slices of cake or pie. Later, the candy was wrapped by hand in tinfoil and advertised as a "Nourishing Lunch for a Nickel."

For nine years, the thick, luscious mounds of candy had no name. When a customer wanted to buy one, he or she had to point it out to the sales clerk.

There are several stories that tell how the Goo Goo Cluster

Factory workers making Goo Goos (Courtesy Standard Candy Company)

finally got its name. One story says that Howell Campbell held a contest to name his candy bar. The contestant who won said the candy should be named "Goo Goo" because "it is so good everyone ought to call for it from birth."

Another story claims that Campbell was in the habit of discussing his candy bar with fellow streetcar passengers every morning on the way to work. He also liked to brag about his wonderful children to anyone who would listen. One morning, on the way into downtown Nashville, he was sitting beside a schoolteacher.

"My son has learned to talk," Campbell told the woman.

"How wonderful! What can he say?"

"Goo-goo," Campbell replied proudly.

"Then that's the name you should give your candy bar!"

No one is sure which, if either, of those two stories is true.

One story that is sometimes told is definitely not true. That story says *Goo* comes from the first letters of the name "Grand Ole Opry." Why can't this story be true? Because Goo Goos were named in

93

1912. It was more than a decade later—in 1925—that the Grand Ole Opry began!

Howell Campbell's son, Howell, Jr., was also in the candy business. After serving in World War II, he returned home to become owner of Huggins Candy Company. Huggins soon merged with Standard Candy Company. By the mid 1950s, Standard had become the biggest candy company in Nashville.

One of the smartest things Howell Campbell, Jr. ever did was to sign Goo Goo Clusters on as a sponsor of the Grand Ole Opry in 1960. Because radio audiences all over the United States listened to the Opry, people far away from Tennessee learned about a candy bar many of them had never heard of before—Goo Goo Clusters!

The Grand Ole Opry is the longest-running live radio program in the United States. It is performed live every Friday and Saturday night from the Opry House in Nashville.

Every year, more than a million people travel from all over the world to attend the Grand Ole Opry. Millions more tune in to radio station WSM 650 AM to listen to the show, which on a clear night can be heard in more than thirty states. Others watch the Saturday night performance on Country Music Television, a cable TV network.

How did the Opry get started? The story begins in the early 1920s with a man named George D. Hay.

Hay was a Memphis newspaperman who became a radio announcer. He started a program called "WLS Barn Dance" at a radio station in Chicago. The show featured live mountain music and soon became quite popular.

Executives at the National Life and Acci-

Standard Candy Company's candies
(Courtesy Standard Candy Company)

dent Insurance Company in Nashville had begun a brand-new radio station named WSM. They talked Hay into coming back to Tennessee to be WSM's program director and chief announcer. However, many of the officials did not agree with the kind of programming Hay wanted to produce.

"Mr. Hay," they said to him. "You must keep in mind that Nashville is considered the Athens of the South. Our citizens are educated and refined. Our listeners will not tolerate hayseed entertainment."

"Gentlemen, I think you are wrong," Hay replied. "Most of the people who listen to WSM and who buy insurance from National Life are working-class, rural people."

"But Nashvillians will insist on lectures and dance orchestras and classical music from our station. They won't like the image mountain music might give of our fair city."

"Just give me a chance," Hay said with a smile. "That's all I ask."

Hay invited Uncle Jimmy Thompson, a seventy-seven-year-old fiddle player from Laguardo, Tennessee, to be his first guest on the "Barn Dance." Thompson claimed to know a thousand tunes by heart, and he played for more than an hour without interruption.

The station was flooded with telephone calls and telegrams. Listeners begged to hear more of this old-time music.

Soon, other fiddle players, banjo pickers, guitar strummers, and even a woman who played a zither were performing regularly on WSM's "Barn Dance."

Audiences loved it. Fans crowded the halls in front of National Life's fifth-floor studio, standing on tiptoe to catch a glimpse of the performers through the tiny studio window.

George Hay had proved that he knew what people wanted to hear. In December 1927, two years after "Barn Dance" began, Hay gave his show a new name. In the time slot that preceded "Barn Dance," WSM broadcast a program of classical music.

"Ladies and gentlemen," Hay said as he opened his show, "for the past hour, you have been listening to music taken largely from 'Grand Opera.' Now you're about to hear the 'Grand Ole Opry.'" The audience was delighted, and the name stuck.

During the very early years of the Opry, all the singers and musicians worked for free. In 1930 the Opry began paying its performers. The starting salary was five dollars a week.

Salesmen for the National Life and Accident Insurance Company gave away Opry tickets to prospective customers. So many people wanted the tickets that the Opry was soon forced to move out of its small studio and into a real theater.

It moved again to a church in east Nashville and then to the War Memorial Auditorium, where Opry executives decided to charge twenty-five cents for admission. Having to pay to see the show didn't keep people from coming. The auditorium was full for nearly every performance.

In 1940, a movie called *Grand Ole Opry* was made in Hollywood. It starred the man who later came to be known as "The King of Country Music"—Roy Acuff. The movie helped people all over the United States to know about the Opry.

By 1943, more than 100 radio stations were broadcasting portions of the Opry to their listeners. Grand Ole Opry performers were now celebrities all over the country.

The Opry moved to the Ryman Auditorium, a sixty-year-old church in downtown Nashville, in 1943. This was to be the Opry's home for the next thirty years. But though the Ryman had nearly 4,000 seats, that wasn't enough to hold all the people who wanted to see the Grand Ole Opry in person.

Ryman Auditorium (Courtesy TSLA)

Going to the Grand Ole Opry was a lot like going to a three-ring circus. In the summer it was hot. There was no air-conditioning, and people tried to keep cool by waving the cardboard funeral-

Onstage at the Grand Ole Opry (Courtesy TSLA)

parlor fans that were given to them when they came in the door. The only heat in the wintertime came from old, creaky cast-iron radiators and the bright lights that shone down onto the stage.

But it wasn't just the temperature that made the Opry like a circus. A hundred things seemed to be going on at once, all the time.

Folks who hadn't been able to get Opry tickets stood outside the Ryman Auditorium on the street and in the alleyway. A few were lucky enough to get spots near the windows and doors, where they could peck in to catch a glimpse of their favorite stars.

Radio audiences could hear the Opry's music and commercials, but there was no way they could possibly imagine what was really going on during the show.

Performers, many of them dressed in outlandish costumes, told jokes, danced, and acted out pantomime routines while commercials were being read. Members of the audience left their seats and came in a steady stream to the edge of the stage to take pictures, ask for autographs, or to make requests for songs.

Customers stood in long lines at the concession stands to buy soft drinks, popcorn, and Goo Goo Clusters.

There were some changes when the Opry moved from the Ryman Auditorium to the new Opry House at Opryland USA in 1974. The new building was state of the art, with sophisticated sound and lighting systems and outstanding acoustics. Central heat and air-conditioning replaced radiators and ceiling fans.

But much about the Opry remained the same. A section of the stage where the lead microphone stood was transplanted from the Ryman to the new site. Several of the Ryman's church-pew seats were moved to the new Opry House. And the performers and their fans were still there.

So were Goo Goo Clusters.

Standard Candy Company had gone through some changes over the years, just as the Opry had. In the same year that the Opry moved out of the Ryman, Howell Campbell, Jr. sold his company.

Things did not go well for the new owners. High interest rates hurt business. A terrible drought in the southeastern United States destroyed almost half of the peanut crop and caused peanut prices to rise sharply. It looked like the Standard Candy Company might have to close its doors.

In 1982, Jimmy Spradley, a young man in his mid twenties, became president of Standard Candy Company. He had some bold new ideas about how to run the business.

"First, I will try to talk big retail chains into stocking Goo Goos," he decided.

Soon, stores like Wal-Mart and Kroger had Goo Goo Clusters in the racks at the checkout lines alongside more famous candy bars. Even upscale department stores like Bloomingdale's in New York City and Marshall Field's & Co. in Chicago sold Goo Goos to their customers.

Spradley persuaded Delta Airlines to give Goo Goos out as flight snacks. Hundreds of thousands of air travelers who had never heard of the candy were now enjoying it and wanting more.

"Once we get people to try Goo Goos, they're hooked," Spradley once said. "There's nothing else like them."

He also added variety to the Goo Goo family, creating Goo Goo Cluster Supreme, which is made with pecans instead of peanuts, and Peanut Butter Goo Goos, which have peanut butter in place of marshmallows. There is even Goo Goo Cluster ice cream.

Spradley knew that one of the most important business moves he could make was to keep advertising on the Opry. "Our candy and the Grand Ole Opry have the same initials," he said. "We won't give up our spot on the show."

Every Saturday night, tens of millions of country music fans listen to the Grand Ole Opry on the radio or watch it on television. There's no way to know how many of those fans enjoy the show while munching on Goo Goos. But it's bound to be a lot.

The two just seem to go together.

Minnie Pearl and Roy Acuff (Courtesy TSLA)

BIBLIOGRAPHY

Country Music Hall of Fame. "Grand Ole Opry." <http://www.countrymusichalloffame.com/hist/grand.ole.opry.html> (July 22, 2002).

Darnell, Catherine. "Standard Candy Company." *The Tennessean*. August 26, 2001.

GooGoo.com. "GooGoo's History." <http://www.googoo.com/history.cfm> (July 22, 2002).

Patterson, Jim. "Country's Flagship, WSM, turns 75." *The Tennessean*. October 8, 2000.

Salomon, Alan. "Opryland sponsors loyal and long term." *Advertising Age*. October 10, 1994.

Wolfe, Charles K. *Tennessee Strings: The Story of Country Music in Tennessee*. Knoxville: University of Tennessee Press, 1977.

Chapter Nine

THE GREATEST SOLDIER OF THEM ALL

Alvin Cullum York Becomes a Hero

"I can't remember a time in my life when I didn't have a gun."

That's one of the most vivid memories that Alvin York, the greatest American soldier of World War I, had about his childhood.

"I sure knew how to use it, too," he said. "My pa would threaten to muss me up right smart if I failed to bring a squirrel down with the first shot or if I hit a turkey in the body instead of taking its head off."

Alvin Cullum York was born in 1887 in the tiny community of Pall Mall, in Fentress County, Tennessee, just seven miles from the Kentucky border. Alvin was the third of William and Mary York's eleven children.

The family lived in a one-room cabin built of rough-hewn logs chinked with sticks and clay. The inside walls were papered with newspapers and colored magazine covers.

William farmed the rocky land that surrounded the cabin. He also worked as a blacksmith. Mary cooked and cleaned and cared for her children. To earn money, she took in other people's laundry. Sometimes, instead of cash, she was paid with worn-out clothes that she altered to fit her own family.

The eight York boys learned to hunt almost as soon as they learned to walk. They knew where wild animals lived and they knew how to stalk and kill them. Hunting wasn't a sport to Alvin and his brothers—it was necessary to provide food for the family table.

Pall Mall, nestled deep in the valley of the Three Forks of the

The York family cabin in Pall Mall, 1929 (Courtesy Alvin York Foundation)

Wolf River, was miles from the nearest main road. Its only school stayed open just three months each year—in winter, after the crops had been harvested and it was too cold and wet to prepare the fields for spring planting.

One teacher conducted lessons and tried to keep order among the dozens of students who crowded the schoolhouse. Boys and girls of all ages sat on backless benches built of split logs and studied from the only two books the school had—a spelling book and the Bible.

"I guess you could say I had a total of nine months of formal education," York wrote. "I made it through the third grade before I quit going to school."

In 1911 Alvin's father died after being kicked in the head by a mule. His mother was left to raise the family alone. Twenty-four-year-old Alvin was her oldest child still living at home. The pressures of being the "man of the family" soon proved too difficult for him to handle. While his younger brothers took care of the farm, Alvin worked in a sawmill and joined a construction crew building a new road through the county.

But on weekends, he partied.

"I drank a lot of moonshine liquor, gambled my wages away,

stayed out late at night, and got in a lot of fistfights," he wrote in his 1928 autobiography. "Deep down in my heart, I knew I was doing things that weren't right, but I just couldn't stop myself."

Though his mother begged him to change his ways, he wouldn't. The pleas of his girlfriend, Gracie Williams, did no good, either. It was not until his best friend was killed in a barroom ruckus that Alvin York gave up the wild life he had been living for almost four years.

On New Year's Day 1915, he attended a church prayer meeting that changed him forever. "When I quit evil, I quit it all," York later recalled. "I have never since drunk whisky or touched cards or smoked or chewed or fought or cussed."

He became a member of the Church of Christ in Christian Union and was soon teaching Sunday school classes and leading the hymn singing with his strong tenor voice. And he began a serious courtship with Gracie.

Even though York had abandoned his wild ways, Gracie's parents did not approve of him. He was almost twice her age and her father considered him "no account," so Alvin and Gracie courted in secret. Alvin would leave home to hunt squirrels in the afternoons at the same time Gracie was driving her family's cattle home. They'd meet on a large flat rock near a grove of beech trees that separated their families' properties.

It was at that spot in 1917 that Gracie accepted Alvin's marriage proposal.

But the wedding would have to wait. The United States had become involved in a war in Europe—a war later known as World War I. In June 1917, York received a letter instructing him to register for the draft.

He later told about his reaction to that letter. "I didn't want to go and kill," he said. "I believed in my Bible and it distinctly said 'Thou Shall Not Kill,' and yet old Uncle Sam wanted me and he said he wanted me most awful bad and I just didn't know what to do."

Both his mother and the pastor from his church urged him not to join the Army. They wanted him to fill out papers to become a *conscientious objector*—a person who refuses to go to war because his religion will not allow it.

That's when he began keeping a diary.

SERGEANT ALVIN C. YORK, WHO WITH SEVEN
COMPANIONS CAPTURED 132 HUNS

Sergeant York, who is an elder of a church in his home town in Tennessee,
recently returned from France, where as leader he carried out one of the
most remarkable exploits of the war—the capture of 132 German soldiers

Alvin C. York in uniform (Courtesy TSLA)

When York received his draft card, he wrote "Dont [sic] want to fight" at the bottom of it.

In his diary he wrote, "I am a soul in doubt. I make up my mind to follow God and the next minute I hesitate and almost make up my mind to follow my country. I want to follow both but I can't. They are opposite. I want to be a good Christian and a good American, too."

York decided to go up a mountainside to find the answer. "I prayed and prayed two whole days and a night, and I received assurance direct from God that it was all right that I should go, and that I would come back without a scratch. I told my little old mother not to worry but it was very hard on her, just like it was on all mothers, and she didn't want to see me go."

In November 1917, Alvin York—a young man who had never traveled more than twenty-five miles from the place he was born—reported for basic training at Fort Gordon, in Georgia. "I had never been out of the mountains before," he wrote, "and I missed them right smart."

York was assigned to the "All-American Division"—a unit made up of soldiers from every state in the Union. Many recruits had been raised in big cities or had recently come to the United States from foreign lands. Before he joined the Army, York had never known anyone who wasn't like himself—a poor white Protestant from rural Tennessee. At first, he was nervous and uncomfortable around his new comrades.

"It was a mixed platoon, with Greeks and Italians and New York

Jews and some Irish," he wrote. "I sure did miss the mountain boys from Tennessee and Kentucky. But I soon got to like those other boys."

Much to York's amazement, some of his fellow soldiers had never before held a gun in their hands.

"Back home in Tennessee, we had just about the best shots that ever squinted down a barrel," he wrote in his diary. "We could shoot the head off a turkey at 150 yards. But some of these city boys don't just miss the targets they're shooting at. They even miss the hills the targets are setting on."

Because of his skills as a marksman, York was soon promoted to corporal and put in charge of teaching new recruits to shoot. In May 1918, York's unit departed for France to fight the Germans.

It was the first time he had ever seen the ocean, and he was seasick. "It was too much water for me," he wrote.

One of the first things York did when he arrived in France was to buy a little black notebook to use as a battle diary. But he soon found out that diaries were against the rules for combat soldiers.

"If the Germans should capture you, your diary could reveal a lot of valuable information we don't want the enemy to know," York's captain told his troops. Then he looked straight at York. "Are you keeping a diary, Corporal York?" he asked.

York didn't even blink. "Sir, I didn't come to this war to be captured. I'm not going to be captured. If the Germans get any information out of me, they'll have to get it out of my dead body," he replied.

The captain turned and walked away. York kept his diary.

None of the new soldiers were prepared for the horrors of war. They spent day after day in muddy, rat-infested trenches. They wore cumbersome masks to protect their lungs from the deadly gas used by enemy troops. Warplanes hummed overhead and grenades constantly exploded around them.

"We stumble over dead horses and dead men and the shells burst all around us," York wrote after his first week on the front. "All through the long nights the big guns flash and growl just like the lightning and thunder when it storms in the mountains at home. . . . And I'm telling you, the little log cabin in Wolf Valley in old Tennessee seems a long way off. . . . We used to do a lot of ducking when those bullets came buzzing around our ears. But soon we realized it was no use. You never hear the one that gets you."

October 8, 1918, was to be a major turning point in the war and in Alvin York's life. He and sixteen other American soldiers were sent that morning to capture a railroad near the Argonne Forest. Because their map was written in French rather than English, they mistakenly ended up behind enemy lines.

The Americans surprised a group of about twenty German soldiers eating breakfast. After a brief firefight, those Germans surrendered. But just minutes later, German machine gunners opened fire on the American soldiers.

"My pals were getting picked off until it looked like none were left," York wrote later in his diary. "We were getting it from the front and both flanks. It was awful. Our boys just went down like the long grass before the mowing machine at home."

Nine Americans soldiers lay wounded or dead, including York's best friend.

"I just knew we couldn't go on until those machine guns were mopped up," York wrote. Remembering his turkey-hunting days, he lay still and waited for the heads of the German soldiers to bob up. Then he shot them.

As a line of German soldiers armed with guns and bayonets rushed toward the Americans, York's hunting experience served him well. With a pistol in one hand and a rifle in the other, he calmly began shooting the soldiers at the back of the line so that those in front would not know what was happening. One after another, the Germans fell dead.

The German commander didn't realize that his troops were battling only a handful of American soldiers. He believed that the situation was hopeless. He blew a whistle and ordered the firing to cease.

Dozens of German soldiers headed down the hill with their hands raised over their heads. The eight able-bodied American soldiers herded their prisoners together and began the long march back to headquarters. Along the way, more German troops surrendered and joined the line of prisoners.

York and his men handed the captives over to Army officials to be counted. There were four German officers and 128 enlisted men.

"Well, Corporal York," the brigade commander said, "I hear you have captured the whole German army."

York saluted. "No, sir," he replied. "I only have 132 of them."

The next morning, American commanders returned to the scene of the battle and found twenty-eight dead German soldiers. York said that was the number of shots he had fired.

French commander Ferdinand Foch called York's heroics "the greatest thing accomplished by any private soldier of all the armies of Europe."

Alvin York was quickly promoted to the rank of sergeant and received many awards for bravery, including the Congressional Medal of Honor, the Distinguished Service Cross, and the French *Croix de Guerre*. He commented modestly that he had no need for so many medals.

"I'd have to have two coats if I wanted to wear them all at the same time," he said.

On November 11, just a little more than a month after the Battle of the Argonne Forest, the armistice ending World War I was signed. In his diary York wrote, "I was glad it was all over. There had been enough fighting and killing and my feelings were like most of the American boys. We were ready to go home."

After touring Paris, where he visited Napoleon's Tomb, Versailles, the Grand Opera, and the Eiffel Tower, York boarded a ship bound for New York. He was not prepared for the welcome that awaited him there.

"They gave me a right sweet reception," he wrote. "They drove me through the streets in an open car. . . . It seemed as though most all of the people knew me and when they began to throw the paper and the ticker tape and the confetti out of the windows of those great big skyscrapers, I wondered what it was at first. It looked just like a blizzard."

York was touched by the welcome. After New York, he visited Washington, D.C. But he wanted to go home. "I wanted to get back to my people where I belonged," he wrote.

In late May 1919, York's train arrived in Crossville. Thousands of well-wishers lined the railroad tracks to catch a glimpse of the hero who had brought the nation's highest war honors back to Tennessee.

York greeted them all. "And then I lit out for the old log cabin

Alvin and Gracie York on their wedding day, 1919 (Courtesy TSLA)

and my little old mother. After that I went to see Gracie. And when I had taken off the uniform and got back into overalls, I went to that place on the mountain where I had prayed before and I thanked the same God who had taken me through the war."

A week after he arrived home, Alvin York married Gracie Williams on the flat rock surrounded by beech trees where they had courted years before. Tennessee governor Albert H. Roberts performed the ceremony under an arch draped with the American flag.

After a honeymoon in Nashville, the couple returned to Pall Mall. They planned to settle down and raise a family in the peace and quiet of the mountains.

But peace and quiet would never be a part of the York family's life. An article in a 1919 issue of *The Saturday Evening Post* magazine had thrust York into the national limelight. The world clamored for his attention.

Offers poured in from Broadway and Hollywood. It seemed that everyone wanted to produce a play or make a movie about Sergeant York. Newspaper reporters begged to write his life story. Businesses pleaded for his endorsement of their products. One gun manufacturer offered York $2,000 if he would fire a single shot while photographers took pictures.

York felt it was wrong to commercialize his fame. He had no interest in the stage or movies, and he was too honest to endorse products he didn't use or like. "I don't deserve money for serving my country," he said as he refused one offer after another.

When all the offers were tallied, Sergeant York had turned down more than half a million dollars!

His one burning desire was to bring education and enlightenment to the people of Fentress County, especially the children.

York's travels had shown him that the isolation which kept many bad things out of the mountains also kept out many good and worthwhile things. His community lacked schools, libraries, good roads, up-to-date houses, and modern farming methods. He vowed to use his newfound fame to change that.

"When I went out into that big world I realized how uneducated I was and what a terrible handicap that is," he said. "I feel called to lead my people toward the chance to get a sensible modern education."

More than one-third of the children in Fentress County did not attend school. One-fifth of the adults in the county couldn't read or write. In 1920 York began a series of lecture tours to raise money for a school. He didn't want to talk about what he had done in the war—he wanted to talk about the importance of learning.

"If I can make a school in my community a reality, I will be prouder of that than anything else I ever did," York said.

In 1926, the Alvin York Industrial and Agricultural Institute opened in a temporary building. Three years later the school moved to a permanent location in Jamestown. York Institute was built on 14,000 beautiful acres and was fully funded and controlled by the state board of education—the only school in Tennessee that had that distinction.

For several years York served as director of the school. When a shortage of funds during the Great Depression threatened to close York Institute, he mortgaged his farm to raise money to pay teachers' salaries, buy school buses, and hire drivers.

In 1936 the board decided that someone with a college degree should run the school. York continued as president emeritus, but he no longer directed day-to-day operations at York Institute.

York turned his attention to farming and to spending more time with Gracie and their eight children. His health was poor, and he had failed to manage his money well. His generous and trusting nature had endeared him to the public, but it had also caused problems for his family and for his business endeavors.

In the late 1930s, filmmaker Jesse Lasky approached York about making a movie telling the story of his life. He refused at first.

"I need to stay home with my family," York said. "Besides, my church doesn't approve of movies. And I still don't think it's right to use what I did in the war to make money for myself."

"But, Mr. York, you would be serving your country by allowing us to make this movie," Lasky replied. "You know what an evil man Hitler is. A movie about you would help persuade Americans that sometimes war is necessary and right. If there are profits, you could use them to build the Bible school you've dreamed of for so many years."

York finally agreed. In July 1941 he attended the premier of the movie *Sergeant York* in New York City. The film won lots of awards. More importantly, it persuaded many Americans that they must get involved in the conflict in Europe and Asia that would soon be known as World War II.

York traveled about the country, speaking in cities and on military bases. "In 1917-1918, we fought for democracy and we saved it for ourselves for twenty-three years," he said. "Now we've got to do it again."

After the United States officially entered the war, York tried to

York attends the premier of the movie *Sergeant York* in New York City, 1941.
(Courtesy TSLA)

enlist in the Army. He was turned away because of poor health. But he spent the war years supporting the Allied cause—giving pep talks to soldiers, raising funds for the Red Cross, leading war-bond drives, and serving as chairman of the Fentress County draft board.

In 1949 York suffered a severe stroke. It was to be followed by two others. By the middle of the 1950s, he was bedridden and almost completely blind. But his mind remained sharp. He never lost interest in what was going on in the world, and he welcomed the many visitors who called on him day after day.

In late summer of 1964, Alvin York was admitted to the Veterans Administration Hospital in Nashville. He died there on September 2 at the age of seventy-six. Though the governor suggested to the family that they allow his body to lie in state at the capitol building, they refused.

"We think it best just to take him back home," his son said.

York's funeral was held at the tiny church—now named York Chapel—which he had founded almost fifty years before. He was buried in the Wolf River cemetery with full military honors.

More than 8,000 people came to pay their last respects to the man whose generosity and whose love of home, family, and country had inspired a nation.

Alvin York's legacy lives on. His home and gristmill in Pall Mall are popular tourist attractions. His statue graces the lawn of the state capitol. The National Guard Armory in Jamestown and the Veterans Hospi-

Statue of Sergeant York on the Tennessee Capitol grounds (Courtesy TSLA)

tal in Murfreesboro bear his name, as does the portion of U.S. Highway 127 that runs through Fentress County.

Most fitting of all, York Elementary School and York Institute continue as living monuments to the man who traded his military fame for educational opportunities for his people.

"What I did in the war is something I want to forget," York often said. "I hope instead that I am remembered for improving education in Tennessee, for bringing in better roads, and just for helping my fellow man."

BIBLIOGRAPHY

Birdwell, Michael. *Celluloid Soldiers: The Warner Bros. Campaign Against Nazism.* New York: New York University Press, 1999.

Birdwell, Michael. "Alvin Cullum York." The Life of Alvin C. York. Jamestown, Tenn.: Alvin C. York Institute. <http://volweb.utk.edu/Schools/York/birdie.html> (July 22, 2002).

Birdwell, Michael. "The Legacy of Alvin C. York." The Life of Alvin C. York. Jamestown, Tenn.: Alvin C. York Institute. <http://volweb.utk.edu/Schools/York/Legacy.html> (July 22, 2002).

Lee, David D. *Sergeant York—An American Hero.* Lexington: University Press of Kentucky, 1985.

Williams, Gladys. "Biography of York." The Life of Alvin C. York. Jamestown, Tenn.: Alvin C. York Institute. <http://volweb.utk.edu/Schools/York/biography.html> (July 22, 2002).

York, Alvin C. "Diary of Sgt. York." The Life of Alvin C. York. Jamestown, Tenn.: Alvin C. York Institute. <http://volweb.utk.edu/Schools/York/diary.html> (July 22, 2002).

Chapter Ten

"VOTE FOR SUFFRAGE, SON!"
A Mother's Letter Gives Women the Vote

August 18, 1920, was a sweltering day in Nashville, Tennessee.
Model-T cars and horse-drawn carriages and throngs of pedes-
trians crowded the brick streets near the state capitol building. Vendors hawked ice cream and cold drinks. Newspaper reporters and
photographers elbowed their way toward the legislative chambers.

The Tennessee General Assembly almost never met during the
summer. Something really big had to be happening for the governor
to call them into special session on a hot week in August.

As young Harry Burn made his way toward his seat in the
House of Representatives, he pulled a handkerchief from his pocket
and wiped the perspiration from his brow. It wasn't just the heat
or the high-collared shirt and wool suit he wore that was making
Harry sweat. He'd never been so nervous in all his life.

Harry Burn was a Republican from McMinn County, in East Tennessee. At age twenty-four, he was the youngest member of the Tennessee House of Representatives. Today he was going to be part of
one of the biggest events in the history of his state and his nation.

He would help decide whether women would be given the right
to vote.

To understand what was going on in Nashville in August of 1920,
it is necessary to go back in history more than seventy years, to a
small church in Seneca Falls, New York. That was where the first
women's rights convention in the United States was held in 1848.

More than 300 men and women met to discuss some very con-
troversial ideas. They talked about the right of women to own property, the right to have equal chances for education and jobs, and

the right to speak out in public.

The most extreme idea to come from the Seneca Falls convention was the notion of *woman suffrage*—the right of women to vote.

Such an idea was shocking to a lot of people, including many women. A woman's place had always been at home, taking care of her husband and children. Women were supposed to let men make all the political decisions.

To allow women to vote would turn the world upside down, or so some people thought.

"Woman suffrage will destroy homes and families," one group of opponents said. "It will result in the end of civilization!"

But some people made it their life's mission to work for equality for women.

Perhaps the most famous suffragist was Susan B. Anthony. Anthony was born in Massachusetts in 1820. From the time she was very young until her death in 1906, she dedicated her life to helping women gain the right to vote.

By the early 1900s, suffragists (or "Suffs" as they were sometimes called) turned their attention to changing the U.S. Constitution. They began to push hard for the passage of what was being called the "Susan B. Anthony Amendment"—an amendment that would guarantee women throughout the country the right to vote.

Suffs wrote letters and met with Senators and Representatives.

They organized huge parades and set up camp on the sidewalks outside the White House lawn. Some even handcuffed themselves to the White House fence.

One group burned a dummy of President Woodrow Wilson to show how unhappy they were that he would not support woman suffrage.

Many of the Suffs were arrested and thrown into dirty, rat-infested jails. Some of them went on hunger strikes, refusing to eat until they were released.

In 1918 the United States entered World War I. One of the reasons President Wilson gave for sending U.S. troops to war was "to make the world safe for democracy."

Suffs had a comment about that: "Why should we send American soldiers to war to help bring democracy to other parts of the world, when half the citizens of the United States do not even have the most basic democratic right—the right to vote?" They also pointed out that twenty-six other nations, including Germany and Russia, already allowed women the vote.

In 1919, President Wilson finally changed his mind and declared that he favored passage of the Susan B. Anthony Amendment.

It was Congress's turn to act. For an amendment to become part of the Constitution, it first must be passed by two-thirds of both houses of Congress. Congress had always said "no" to the idea of woman suffrage. What would this Congress do?

It didn't take long to find out. In May of 1919, the U.S. House of Representatives narrowly voted in favor of woman suffrage. A few days later the U.S. Senate approved the measure by a margin of only one vote.

Suffs throughout the nation held joyous celebrations. But they knew their work was far from over. Now the Suffs had to persuade the legislatures in at least thirty-six states to ratify (approve) the Susan B. Anthony Amendment.

Six states quickly approved the amendment. By February of 1920, thirty-two states had jumped on the ratification bandwagon. Oklahoma became number thirty-three. West Virginia was thirty-fourth, followed by the state of Washington. Would there be a "Magic Thirty-Sixth"? Which state would it be?

Suffs pinned their hopes on Delaware. But when the amendment was defeated there, they turned their eyes South—to Tennessee.

The battle for women's rights had been raging in Tennessee for almost as long as it had been going on in the rest of the country. Susan B. Anthony herself had visited the state in the late 1800s to speak in favor of woman suffrage. In 1919, the General Assembly gave women the right to vote in local and in presidential elections. But women were still not allowed a voice in state politics.

People who were against woman suffrage were called *Anti-Suffragists*, or *Antis*. They claimed that most women in Tennessee did not wish to vote and that they preferred to leave politics and government business to the "wisdom of the men."

Many Antis believed that woman suffrage would destroy homes and families and that it would make women masculine and men feminine. They adopted slogans that said, "A vote for federal suffrage is a vote for organized female nagging forever," and "Don't

HOME!

An anti-suffrage cartoon (Courtesy TSLA)

give women what they want—give them what they ought to have!" and "Let the women pray and the men vote."

Illustrators who supported the anti-suffrage cause were busy in 1920. One popular drawing of the day shows a man coming home from work to find his two young children alone and crying. Draped across a wall in the kitchen is a banner that reads VOTES FOR WOMEN, with a note pinned to it. "Back some time this evening," the note says.

Another illustration shows a hen wearing a VOTES FOR WOMEN ribbon, walking away from her nest of eggs. The rooster says, "Why, Ma, these eggs will get all cold!" The hen replies, "Set on them yourself, Old Man, my country calls me!"

Suffs were busy promoting their cause, too. One of their most popular spokespersons was a Nashville woman named Anne Dallas Dudley. Dudley came from a wealthy, prominent family. She was beautiful and very ladylike. A photograph of her reading to her two young daughters was used to attack the notion that Suffs were mannish and anti-family.

"Women must be involved in politics because politics affects family life," Dudley often said. In response to an Anti remark that "only those who bear arms should vote," Dudley said, "Men may bear arms, but women bear armies."

Tennessee Governor Albert H. Roberts agreed to call the General Assembly into special session in August of 1920 to consider ratifi-

Anne Dallas Dudley with her daughters
(Courtesy TSLA)

cation of the Nineteenth Amendment. That's why Harry Burn and the other legislators were in Nashville.

Suffs and Antis went to work. Both groups set up headquarters in the fancy new Hermitage Hotel in downtown Nashville. The hotel was near the state capitol building, and many legislators stayed there while the General Assembly was in session.

In an attempt to predict the outcome of the vote, campaigners for both sides of the issue had asked every legislator to state his position on woman suffrage. They all knew, however, that their counts were probably not accurate; some legislators were likely to lie, and some would change their minds even after promising a vote.

There was no way to know how any lawmaker would vote until the official roll call was taken.

As time for the vote drew near, the hotel and the capitol began to bloom like a flower garden. Antis handed out red roses to legislators who promised to vote against suffrage. Suffs gave yellow roses to their supporters. Not every member of the General Assembly wore a rose in the buttonhole of his lapel, but most did.

On August 13, the Tennessee Senate ratified the suffrage amendment by a vote of twenty-five to four. Suffs were happy, but they had expected that to happen. It was far too early to celebrate.

The real fight would be in the House of Representatives.

Suffs knew they had to protect every single vote that had been promised them. They couldn't allow the Antis an opportunity to change the minds of pro-suffrage legislators. So they took their representatives for long walks. They took them for drives in the country. They took them to movies. They took them to dinner.

Anti-suffragists at the Hermitage Hotel (Courtesy TSLA)

Antis sent fake messages to some pro-suffrage lawmakers, telling them of illnesses in their families or other emergencies that would summon them home and keep them from voting.

To keep their supporters from sneaking out in the middle of the night, Suffs patrolled the halls of the Hermitage Hotel and posted guards at the Nashville train station.

On the morning of August 18, ninety-six of the ninety-nine members of the Tennessee House of Representatives were present when the meeting was called to order.

Some had made a special effort to be there. One legislator had cut short a trip to California so that he could cast his vote in favor of suffrage. Another representative had just been released from the hospital, where he had told his doctor, "If I live, I'm going to be in Nashville to vote for woman suffrage!"

Forty-nine votes were needed to pass the amendment. Suffs were pretty sure they could count on forty-eight, but that wasn't enough. A tie vote would kill the amendment. Was there a number forty-nine? Who would he be?

The Speaker of the House banged his gavel. "The hour has come!" he said.

The alphabetical roll call vote began. The first two legislators voted "aye." The next four voted "nay."

Then it was Harry Burn's turn. Most people were sure they knew how he would vote. Stuck securely in the buttonhole of Harry's lapel was a bright red rose. Suffs knew that he came from a county where many people were against woman suffrage. They thought that because he was so young

Representative Harry Burn
(Courtesy McClung Historical Collection)

and inexperienced, it had been easy for the Antis to bribe or bully him into voting "nay."

What nobody but Harry knew was that he had something tucked in his coat pocket, right next to his heart, that was much more important than the color of the flower he wore. It was a letter—a letter from his mother.

> Dear Son:
> Hurrah, and vote for suffrage! Don't keep them in doubt. I noticed some of the speeches against. They were bitter. I have been watching to see how you stood, but have not noticed anything yet. Don't forget to be a good boy and help Mrs. Catt [a prominent suffrage leader] put the "rat" in ratification.
>
> Signed,
> Your Mother

When Harry's name was called, he spoke softly. "Aye," he said.

People in the crowd couldn't believe their ears. Many shook their heads in wonder. It was still too early for the Suffs to celebrate. But when the roll call was finished, everyone realized that Harry Burn's vote had tipped the scales in favor of ratification.

Women began weeping and screaming. Suffs threw their arms around each other and began to dance. Antis, shouting and waving their fists, swarmed toward Harry. "Bribery!" they cried. "Harry Burn's been bribed!"

Harry was scared to death. He looked around for a place to hide. Spotting an open window, he clambered through it and found himself on a narrow third-floor ledge. Gripping the rough stone wall and gingerly edging his way along, he finally came to an unlocked attic window. He crawled in and hid in the stifling heat for a while; then he strolled back to the lobby and melted anonymously into the crowd.

Governor Roberts signed and sealed Tennessee's certificate of ratification and sent it to Washington, D.C.

On August 26, 1920, the Susan B. Anthony Amendment officially became the nineteenth amendment to the U.S. Constitution. The

Picture from the *Nashville Tennessean* of Governor Roberts as he signs the ratification bill (Courtesy TSLA)

seventy-two-year battle for woman suffrage was over. At last, women had gained the right to vote in every election in every state in the nation.

And Tennessee had won its place in history as the state that made it possible.

BIBLIOGRAPHY

Sims, Anastatia. "'Powers That Pray' and 'Powers That Prey': Tennessee and the Fight for Woman Suffrage." *Tennessee Historical Quarterly 50*, no. 4 (1991): 203-225.

Taylor, A. Elizabeth. "The Woman Suffrage Movement in Tennessee." Ph. D. diss., Vanderbilt University, 1943. New York: Bookman, 1957.

Chapter Eleven

MONKEYING AROUND WITH EVOLUTION
John Scopes Goes on Trial

The high school football coach was on trial.

It was July 1925 in Dayton, Tennessee, a small town in the south-eastern part of the state. The trial that was taking place at the Rhea County courthouse in the center of town was to become one of the most famous in United States history.

The coach's name was John Scopes. He was twenty-four years old and a first-year math and physics teacher at Rhea County High School. He wasn't in trouble for anything he had done on the football field. Instead, he was accused of breaking the law in his classroom.

That spring, the Tennessee General Assembly had passed a law called the Butler Act. The law made it illegal for teachers in Tennessee public schools to teach "any theory that denies the story of the Divine Creation of man as taught in the Bible, and to teach instead that man has descended from a lower order of animals."

One afternoon in early summer, Scopes was asked to stop by Robinson's Drugstore in downtown Dayton. When he arrived, he found several of the town's prominent businessmen waiting to talk to him. One of them was Fred Robinson, who owned the store and who was president of the Rhea County Board of Education.

"John, my boy, come in and have a seat," Robinson said as Scopes entered the store. "We've got something important to talk about with you."

"What is it, sir?" Scopes tried hard to keep his voice from quiv-

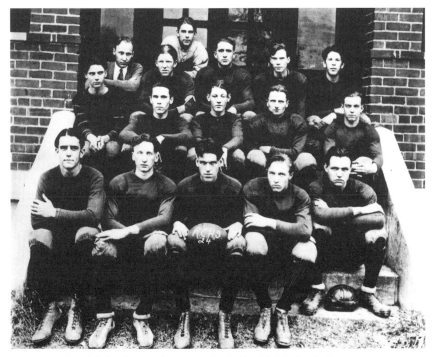

Coach John Scopes (top row, far left) with his football team at
Rhea County High School (Courtesy TSLA)

ering. Was he in trouble with the school board?

Robinson spread a copy of the *Chattanooga Times* on the table in front of them. "Take a look at this ad in this morning's newspaper, John. The American Civil Liberties Union—you know, the ACLU— is trying to find a teacher in Tennessee who is willing to go to court for violating the Butler Act."

"Mr. Robinson, why are you telling me this? To violate the Butler Act, a teacher would have to discuss the theory of evolution. That's taught in biology class, not in the classes I teach."

"Didn't you substitute when the regular biology teacher was sick last term?"

"Yes, sir, I did. But I don't recall whether I discussed evolution."

"Do you remember what textbook you used, John?"

"Of course I do, Mr. Robinson. It was George William Hunter's *Civic Biology*. The same book you're selling right over there." Scopes pointed to a set of bookshelves in the corner of the store.

"Do you have any idea what that book has to say about how

Dayton businessmen—George W. Rappelyea, Walter White, Clay Green, T. Owen
Wasson, and F. E. Robinson—meet at Robinson's Drugstore. (Courtesy TSLA)

human beings came into existence?"

"It goes along with Charles Darwin's *On the Origin of Species*.
Darwin believed that all forms of life evolved over long periods of
time from lower life forms. He believed that human beings developed over the course of millions of years. He believed that monkeys
and humans have common ancestors."

"What do you think about that, John?"

"Mr. Robinson, I believe that all biology teachers have an acade-
mic responsibility to discuss the theory of evolution with their students. I don't think it's possible to teach biology without teaching
Darwin."

"So what do you think of the Butler Act?"

"I think it's a bad law. It takes away teachers' right to teach, and
students' right to learn."

"Then would you be willing to challenge the law in court?"

"Why do you want me to do this? Why not ask the real biology
teacher?"

"Because he might not want to take this risk. He has a wife and children to consider. This trial could drag on for a long time. And it's likely to have some big repercussions. We'd rather not put a family man in such a position."

One of the other men spoke. "John, this town is drying up. Businesses are closing and people are moving away. We have less than 2,000 people living here now. If we can attract attention to Dayton, all that might change. A big, important trial will bring people and their money here."

"There's nothing like publicity to draw new industry to a town," another man said.

"An important trial will be good for business," added another.

Fred Robinson spoke up. "The ACLU will pay all your trial expenses, John. You'll be fighting a law you don't like, and helping your town, too. Say you'll do it."

John Scopes swallowed hard. "Okay," he said softly. "Arrest me."

News that Scopes had agreed to be tried spread quickly, not just in Tennessee, but also throughout much of the country. At stake was more than what one young teacher might have said to a classroom of students. Many people were interested in the Scopes trial as a contest between religion and science.

One of those people was a man from Nebraska named William Jennings Bryan. Bryan was a sixty-five-year-old lawyer who was famous throughout the United States. He had run for President three times.

William Jennings Bryan
(Courtesy TSLA)

He had served one term as Secretary of State. He had spent the last several years traveling all over the country giving impassioned speeches. Audiences were often held spellbound when Bryan spoke.

Bryan's favorite topic was religion. He was a *fundamentalist*, a person who believes every single word in the Bible is literally true.

"The book of Genesis says that God created human beings in one day and that He caused each creature to bring forth its own kind," Bryan often said. "Therefore, Darwin's theory of evolution must be wrong. It is a dangerous, wicked, and immoral idea that must not be taught to our schoolchildren!"

Bryan was eager to get involved with the case of a Tennessee schoolteacher who was going to court for teaching evolution. So eager, in fact, that he offered his services for free. He would travel to Dayton and join with other attorneys to prosecute John Scopes for violating the Butler Act.

That's when another nationally famous lawyer became involved in the trial—Clarence Darrow, a sixty-eight-year-old attorney from Chicago. Darrow was an *agnostic*, a person who is not committed to believing in either the existence or the nonexistence of God. He thought it was wrong to deny teachers and students the right to discuss scientific theories such as evolution in public school.

Clarence Darrow
(Courtesy TSLA)

"The First Amendment to the U.S. Constitution guarantees freedom of speech to everyone, including schoolteachers," Darrow said. "And it also insists on the separation of church and state in our classrooms."

Darrow usually charged tens of thousands of dollars to fight a case. He had never before worked for free, but when he learned that William Jennings Bryan was donating his legal services to the prosecution, Darrow agreed to travel to Dayton to aid the defense team at no charge.

The men at Robinson's drugstore had been right when they said a big trial would bring lots of people to Dayton. In the days before and during the trial, the town looked more like a giant carnival than a site where serious legal matters were taking place.

People wore buttons that said YOUR OLD MAN'S A MONKEY! pinned to their clothes. Teenage girls strolled through town carrying toy monkeys under their arms. Young children begged their parents to let them take pony rides with a real live monkey. A policeman displayed a sign that said MONKEYVILLE POLICE on his motorcycle.

An organ grinder with a pair of dancing monkeys entertained passersby on a street corner. Posters of monkeys were taped to grocery store windows. One soda fountain featured a live chimpanzee sitting on a barstool, sipping a cold drink called "Monkey Fizz."

Street vendors set up shop on every corner. Some used their cars or horse-drawn wagons as temporary stores. Everything imagin-

Dayton teenagers Dee Robinson and Marguarite Parser with toy monkeys.
(Courtesy TSLA)

Rhea County Courthouse (Courtesy TSLA)

able was for sale—from food to monkey souvenirs to Bibles. Thousands of people poured into town from the surrounding countryside to be part of the festivities.

More than a hundred newspaper and magazine reporters and dozens of telegraph operators descended on the little town in the days before the trial.

Chicago radio station WGN set up microphones in the courtroom and broadcast the proceedings live to stations all across the United States. For the first time ever, Americans could follow a trial as it was taking place. Newsreels—short news reports shown in movie theaters—told the nation about "The Monkey Trial That Rocked America."

The Rhea County courthouse had the biggest courtroom in the state of Tennessee. It could hold hundreds of people, but far more than that wanted to watch the Scopes Trial. Crowds stood in the halls and filled the wide stairway. Judge John Raulston ordered that loudspeakers be installed and bleachers built on the courthouse lawn so that people outdoors could listen to the trial.

The weather in Dayton that July was sweltering hot. The summer sun beat down relentlessly on the copper roof of the courthouse, raising temperatures inside to more than 100 degrees. Spectators blocked the floor-to-ceiling windows so that not a hint of a breeze entered the room. The palm-leaf hand fans distributed by local businesses offered little relief. The judge allowed trial participants to shed their coats, ties, and shirt collars, but that didn't help much.

The first order of business was to formally accuse John Scopes of breaking the law. Then a jury had to be selected. At last, it was time for testimony to begin.

Clarence Darrow and the other defense lawyers believed from the beginning that it was going to be difficult for Scopes to receive a fair trial. They worried that religious forces in Dayton were just too strong.

Huge banners displayed about town said READ YOUR BIBLE. Preachers stood on street corners and warned passersby of the wickedness of "evil-ution." The judge himself carried a Bible under his arm to court every morning and allowed each session to be opened with a prayer. Some of the jurors admitted that the Bible was the only book they had ever read. None of them seemed to know much about Darwin's theory of evolution.

The prosecutors—attorneys who were trying to prove that Scopes had broken the law—called the Rhea County superintendent of schools to the stand.

"Yes," he said. "John Scopes admitted to teaching Charles Darwin's theories."

Two boys who had been in biology class when Scopes was the substitute teacher were called to testify. They liked the teacher and did not want to get him in trouble, but they knew they had to tell the truth. "Yes," they said. "Mr. Scopes taught from a book that discusses evolution."

"We have proved the defendant's guilt," the prosecuting attorneys said. "We rest our case."

It appeared as though the trial might be over before it had scarcely begun. Both William Jennings Bryan and Clarence Darrow were disappointed. They had hoped that bigger issues than Scopes's guilt or innocence would be raised. They wanted to talk about evolution and religion, and about whether the government has a right to tell teachers what to say in their classrooms.

The next afternoon Bryan showed that he was not willing to let the trial end so quickly and quietly. He stood before the court with a copy of Hunter's *Civic Biology* textbook in his hand. He pointed out a diagram that showed humans lumped together with other mammals.

"How dare scientists put man with lions and tigers and everything that is bad!" he exclaimed. "Parents have a right to say that no public school teacher shall rob their children of faith in God by

Bryan speaks in the crowded courtroom. (Courtesy TSLA)

teaching such things."

Defense attorney Dudley Malone, one of Scopes's lawyers, had a reply to that. "The defense wishes to show that evolution does not mock Christianity," he said. "Why does the prosecution fear the teaching of science? Let the children have their minds kept open."

Darrow and his team of attorneys had brought scientists and clergymen from around the country to Dayton as expert witnesses in the case. They wanted to show that the teaching of evolution did not need to destroy religious faith. They hoped that these experts could educate the court and the public about evolution. They would try to convince the jury that it was important that Darwin's theory be taught in high school biology classes.

But the prosecution argued that the only issue in the trial was whether John Scopes had broken the law. Judge Raulston agreed. He would not allow the defense's experts to testify before the jury, but he did allow their opinions to be part of the official trial transcript.

On July 20, ten days after the trial had begun, the judge made a surprise announcement. "I fear that this courtroom floor may cave in due to excessive weight," he said. "And the temperature in here is more than any of us can stand. I am moving the trial outside to the courthouse lawn." And he did.

Then something even more surprising happened. The defense attorneys called William Jennings Bryan to the stand to testify.

"We object!" the prosecuting attorneys cried in unison.

But Bryan held up his hand to quiet them. "I welcome the opportunity to defend traditional religion against the forces of Godlessness," he said. "I am happy to testify."

Darrow began his questioning. He asked whether Bryan considered himself an expert on the Bible.

"Yes, I have studied the Bible for about fifty years," Bryan replied.

"Do you believe that everything in the Bible should be literally interpreted?" Darrow asked.

"I believe everything in the Bible should be accepted as given," Bryan replied.

Darrow then went on to question Bryan about several stories from the Bible. He asked him whether he believed Eve was created from Adam's rib. He asked him where Cain found a wife. He asked him about Noah and the great flood. He asked him whether Joshua really made the earth stand still and if he believed that a big fish swallowed Jonah.

"I accept each of these biblical miracles on faith," Bryan replied.

Then Darrow began to ask about the creation story found in the Bible. "Do you think the days described in Genesis were twenty-four-hour days?"

"My impression is that they were periods," Bryan replied.

"Do you think that the creation may have been going on for a very long time?"

"It might have continued for millions of years."

Many of the fundamentalists in the crowd gasped. If a "day" could be defined as a "period," then the theory of evolution might be valid.

Bryan's face grew red. "Mr. Darrow, you are trying to slur at the Bible."

Darrow's face was red, too. "I am examining you on your fool ideas that no intelligent Christian on earth believes."

People in the crowd began shouting in anger. Judge Raulston feared that a riot might break out. He banged his gavel. "This court is adjourned for the day!"

It was July 21, 1925. Judge Raulston opened court by declaring that Bryan's testimony from the day before had no bearing on John Scopes's guilt or innocence. It was to be struck from the record and the jury was not allowed to consider it.

"Your only job," he told the members of the jury, "is to decide whether the defendant taught that man is descended from a lower order of animals."

The jury deliberated only nine minutes before agreeing that Scopes had violated the Butler Act. "We find the defendant guilty," the jury foreman said.

"Very well," said the judge. "I set the fine at $100. Court is dismissed."

The "Great Monkey Trial" officially came to an end twelve days after it had begun.

Souvenir stands were taken down. Vendors stopped selling hot dogs, popcorn, and cold drinks and went back to their regular jobs. Wandering evangelists went elsewhere to preach. Not one live monkey or chimpanzee could be found in all of Rhea County.

Clarence Darrow returned to his law practice in Chicago.

William Jennings Bryan spent five days following the trial's end giving speeches in towns near Dayton. He lay down to take a nap after Sunday dinner and died in his sleep, probably as the result of a stroke.

Although John Scopes could have remained in his teaching job at Rhea County High School, he chose instead to go to the University of Chicago, where he earned a master's degree in geology. He then took a job with an oil company. In 1960, he returned to Dayton to attend the premier of the movie *Inherit the Wind*, a story loosely based on the trial that bore his name.

Dayton never did grow into the bustling activity center the men at Robinson's drugstore had hoped for. It remains a small town in the Tennessee River Valley.

The majestic Rhea County courthouse, still in use today, stands in the middle of the town square. The basement houses the Scopes Trial Museum, which is free and open to the public. Just a couple of miles from the courthouse is Bryan College, a fundamentalist Christian institution founded in 1930 in memory of William Jennings Bryan.

John Scopes's conviction was appealed to the Tennessee Supreme

Court in 1926. That court overturned the guilty verdict because the judge rather than the jury had imposed the fine. That meant that the case could not be appealed to a higher court. The Butler Act remained law until 1967, when the Tennessee General Assembly repealed it.

People all over the country still disagree about whether Darwin's theory of evolution should be taught in public schools. Many still see the issue as a struggle between religion and science.

And every time the question arises, people remember the famous Scopes Monkey Trial that took place in 1925 in Dayton, Tennessee.

BIBLIOGRAPHY

Blake, Arthur. *The Scopes Trial: Defending the Right to Teach*. Brookfield, Conn.: Millbrook Press, 1994.

Chadwick, Bruce. *Infamous Trials*. edited by Austin Sarat. Crime Series. Broomall, Penn.: Chelsea House, 1997.

Edward J. Larson. *Summer for the Gods: The Scopes Trial and America's Continuing Debate over Science and Religion*. New York: Basic Books, 1997.

Mercer, Theodore C. ed. 1990. *The World's Most Famous Court Trial: Tennessee Evolution Case*. Dayton, Tenn.: Bryan College, 1990. Original edition, Cincinatti: National Book Company, 1925.

Webb, George E. *The Evolution Controversy in America*. Lexington: University of Kentucky Press, 1994.

Chapter Twelve

ON TOP OF OLD SMOKY

The USA's Most Popular National Park

Park entrance (Courtesy Great Smoky Mountains National Park)

It was almost midnight, but the campground in the Great Smoky Mountains wasn't quiet. Brandon lay awake, listening to noises very different from the ones he heard in the city.

No car motors raced. No telephones rang. No sirens wailed. No radios blared. No horns honked. Frogs sang and crickets chirped and the river gurgled over the rocks.

Beside him in the tent, Brandon's dad snored contentedly.

Brandon should have been tired enough to fall asleep. That morning, he and his dad had visited Newfound Gap. His dad had taken a picture of him standing with one foot in Tennessee and the other in North Carolina. Then they'd hiked to Clingman's Dome, the highest point in the Smoky Mountains.

After that, they drove to Elkmont campground and pitched their tent. They built a campfire and cooked hot dogs and beans. Soon after the sun went down, they crawled into their tent and snuggled into their sleeping bags.

The next day they were going to rent bicycles and ride through Cades Cove, a restored pioneer settlement filled with historical log cabins, farm buildings, and churches. Then they were going to go trout fishing.

Outside the tent the October air was chilly, but it was cozy and warm inside. Brandon's eyelids began to grow heavy. But just as he was about to drift off to sleep, he heard something moving around the campsite. Leaves crunched and twigs broke, and there was the sound of heavy breathing.

"Dad," he whispered. "Wake up!"

His father just snored.

"Dad!" Brandon shook his father's shoulder. "There's something out there."

His father opened one eye. "Go to sleep, Brandon."

"But, Dad, listen!"

The noises grew louder and Brandon's heart beat fast. His dad's eyes were wide open now. "It's probably just a raccoon or a possum," he said.

"Or maybe a skunk," Brandon added, hoping he was wrong.

"Good thing we locked the food in the trunk of the car."

"Yeah, good thing."

Brandon closed his eyes. He wasn't afraid of raccoons or possums, or even skunks. When the intruder discovered there was nothing to eat at the campsite, it would go away.

Then the animal growled.

His father sat bolt upright. "Hand me the flashlight, son." He lifted the tent flap and shined the beam into the darkness. A huge black bear was walking round and round their car.

"Dad . . . what are we going to do?" Brandon was trying hard to keep his voice from trembling.

"We're not going to do anything. Just lie still and be quiet."

The bear stood on its hind legs and pawed at the car windows. It climbed onto the hood of the car and then onto the roof. The bear lifted its face to the sky and growled. Then it jumped down and

Smoky Mountain black bear
(Photo by Karl and Susie Klein)

lumbered off into the woods.

For the first time in what seemed like hours, Brandon began to breathe easily again. But he had a feeling that neither he nor his dad was going to get much sleep that night.

Brandon and his dad were just two of the more than ten million people who visit the Great Smoky Mountains National Park every year. The park is located on the border between Tennessee and North Carolina, within a day's drive of one-third of the people who live in the United States.

The Great Smoky Mountains National Park receives more visitors than the Grand Canyon or Yellowstone or Yosemite parks. In fact, more people visit the Smoky Mountains each year than all other national parks combined.

Tourists come to the Smokies for many reasons—to camp, to hike, to fish, to watch wildlife, or to learn about the Cherokee Indians and white pioneers who once lived on the land. Many come

Cherokees called these mountains "the place of blue smoke."
(Photo by Karl and Susie Klein)

simply to relax beneath the canopy of the Smokies' tall trees and let nature soothe their troubles away.

The Great Smoky Mountains are part of the southern Appalachian mountain range. Geologists believe they are millions of years old—far older than the Rocky Mountains in the western United States. Countless centuries of wind, water, and time have rounded the jagged peaks of the Smokies so that today they look far different than most of the world's other mountain ranges.

Tribes of Indians, called Cherokees, first lived in these mountains about 1,000 years ago. For hundreds of years they hunted, fished, and farmed in the hills they called "Shaconage" (sha-CON-a-gay)—the place of blue smoke.

The mist that originally gave the mountains their name is caused by *transpiration*—the process by which plants exhale vapor through their leaves. That is the blue smoke the Cherokees talked about.

European explorers first invaded Cherokee territory in the 1500s, followed by hunters, trappers, and traders. These men took care of business and then returned to their homes east of the mountains. Because they were not interested in claiming Indian lands, their

137

relationships with the Cherokees were usually peaceful and friendly.

But in the late 1700s that began to change.

Settlers—people who built homes, raised families, and stayed on the land—began to move into the area in great numbers. Some of these settlers wanted to live in peace with the Indians, but many of them did not. They fought the Cherokees, and, in time, persuaded them to sign treaties giving up tribal lands.

In 1830, the U.S. Congress passed the Indian Removal Act, which ordered Indians who lived east of the Mississippi River to give up their lands and move west. Many Cherokees refused to obey the law. In 1838, the U.S. Army rounded up almost 16,000 of them and forced them to move to Oklahoma. More than 4,000 Indians died on the journey now known as the Trail of Tears.

Not all of the Cherokees went west. Several hundred escaped from the soldiers and hid in the mountains. These Indians are known as the Eastern Band of Cherokees. They eventually settled on the Qualla Indian Reservation, near the town of Cherokee, North Carolina. More than 5,000 Cherokees now live there.

A settler's cabin in Cades Cove (Photo by Karl and Susie Klein)

The first white settlers who moved into the Smoky Mountains settled in the coves, where the land was fertile and easy to farm.

Those who came later had a tougher time making a living. Many of them had to settle on mountain slopes, where the soil was thin and rocky and difficult to farm. Some of these "hardscrabble farmers" claimed their fields were so steep that the only way to sow seeds was to stand on an opposite hill and shoot the seeds into the dirt with a shotgun!

Although life was hard for most mountain people, they seldom complained. They hunted for and grew their own food, built their own homes, wove their own cloth, and sewed their own clothes. They delivered their babies without a doctor and buried their dead without an undertaker.

Mountain people learned to "make do or do without." Surrounded by friends and family and breathtaking natural beauty, few of them would have described themselves as poor.

The twentieth century brought huge changes to life in the Smoky Mountains. Lumber companies from the north were searching for more timber to supply the nation's growing demand for building materials.

"Gentlemen, we've cut down the trees in New England and around the Great Lakes," a lumber executive said to his board of directors. "Now we need to turn our attention south, to the forests of Appalachia."

"But those trees will be much too difficult to harvest," a board member replied. "The mountains are steep, and there's no transportation system. And what makes you think that land is for sale?"

"Ah . . . you don't understand. Most of the people who live in those mountains are dirt poor. They'll be eager to sell us their land. And they'll jump at the chance to take jobs building roads and laying rails and cutting trees."

He was right. Beginning in 1901, lumber companies began buying vast tracts of land in the southern Appalachian Mountains. They set up operations that hired hundreds of unemployed mountain men. Then they began stripping the forest of its trees. Maple, birch, chestnut, oak, basswood, and the most prized tree of all—the yellow poplar—fell victim to the loggers' axes and saws.

Backwoods settlements soon became bustling logging towns,

complete with stores, boardinghouses, and sawmills. Trains carried lumberjacks to the tops of the mountains, where they chopped down trees that were hundreds of years old.

Some of the logs were carried down the mountains by rail. Others were removed on *skidders*—large wooden sleds pulled by horses and mules. Many of the giant logs were simply rolled down the mountain, where they crushed and destroyed all vegetation in their path.

Within twenty years, two-thirds of the trees in the Smoky Mountains were gone. Fire had destroyed much of the underlying shrubs and flowers. Mountain streams which once ran clear and pure were murky and clogged with mud and debris. Forest animals sought homes elsewhere. An area that was once a place of indescribable beauty had become a scene from a nightmare.

"The logging must be stopped!"

That's what a group of people from Knoxville said when they witnessed the devastation. Two of those people, Mr. and Mrs. Willis Davis, had visited several national parks in the West.

"Why couldn't we have a national park in the Smokies?" they began to ask.

In 1923 the Great Smoky Mountains Conservation Association was formed. Its mission was to persuade the United States Government to turn the Smoky Mountains into a national park, protected forever from logging and overdevelopment.

It wasn't easy. Unlike national park land in the West, which was already owned by the federal government, land in the Smoky Mountains was privately owned. Eighteen lumber companies and more than 6,000 individuals owned property in the Smoky Mountains. Many of those owners did not want to sell.

"My family has lived in this cove for generations," farmers said. "We're not leaving!"

"There are still thousands of acres of trees to be harvested in these mountains," logging executives said. "We're not leaving!"

"We've hunted these woods, fished these streams, and operated moonshine stills in these hills all our lives," other mountain people said. "We're not leaving!"

There was also the problem of raising enough money to buy the land. It was going to cost more than $12,000,000 to buy the acreage for the park. Where would the money come from?

The state governments of Tennessee and North Carolina believed that a national park would boost tourism in their states, so they each gave $2,500,000. The federal government contributed another $2,000,000.

Private individuals, including hundreds of schoolchildren who dropped hard-earned pennies, nickels, and dimes into jars on their teachers' desks, gave another million.

But it wasn't enough. The fund was still $5,000,000 short of what was needed to purchase land for the park. Then John D. Rockefeller, Jr. stepped in. The Rockefellers were one of the richest families in the world. They had always been interested in nature and conservation. Rockefeller agreed to donate the balance needed to purchase land for the park, in memory of his mother.

With almost $13,000,000 collected, creation of the Great Smoky Mountains National Park began. Most landowners eventually agreed to sell. The government allowed people who didn't want to move from their homes the right to lease them and live there for the rest of their lives. Some of those people remained in the park until the very end of the twentieth century.

President Roosevelt dedicates the park, 1940. (Courtesy GSMNPL)

Once the logging stopped and the forest was left alone, nature began to repair itself. The trees that remained grew bigger. Birds and other animals dropped seeds that soon grew into healthy saplings. Shrubs and wildflowers appeared once more.

In 1934, the U.S. Congress formally established the Great Smoky Mountains National Park. On Labor Day in 1940, President Franklin D. Roosevelt stood at the Rockefeller Memorial, a crescent-shaped rock wall at Newfound Gap.

"We meet today to dedicate the mountains, streams, and forests to the service of the American people," he said.

What a park it is! Forty miles long by twenty miles wide, the 500,000 acres that make up the Great Smoky Mountains National Park contain an abundance and variety of life more diverse than anyplace else in North America.

A breathtaking array of trees, flowering plants, birds, fish, amphibians, and reptiles (including twenty-seven different kinds of salamanders) greets visitors to the Great Smoky Mountains National Park.

The wildlife that many tourists enjoy best are mammals—tiny chipmunks, flying squirrels, groundhogs, foxes, skunks, raccoons, possums, and white-tailed deer. The favorite is the animal that symbolizes the Great Smoky Mountains—the black bear—the same kind of bear that was prowling around Brandon's tent on his first night of camping.

"Dad, did bears live here during the time of the Cherokees and the pioneers?" Brandon asked.

"Yes, son, they did. And lots of other animals were here, too, although some of them aren't around anymore. Bison and wolves were hunted until they were all gone. So were the elk, but the National Park Service is trying to bring them back to the park. And some of the wildlife that lives in the park now really isn't supposed to be here."

"Like what?"

"Some of trout we're hoping to catch tomorrow are not native to the Smokies' streams. The speckled brook trout is really the only one that belongs here, but in the early 1900s, some folks released rainbow trout and brown trout into the streams to improve the fishing."

"Did that hurt the speckled trout?"

Fisherman in Smoky Mountain trout stream (Photo by Karl and Susie Klein)

"Yes it did. The new fish are bigger and stronger, and they eat food and take up space the speckled trout need in order to survive. And there's another animal that doesn't belong in the park that's a lot bigger and more destructive than trout."

"What is it?"

"It's a kind of pig called a wild boar. About a hundred years ago, some people built a hunting reserve here in the mountains. They stocked it with dozens of wild boars, which soon broke out of their pens and escaped. Thousands of their offspring live in the park now."

"Have you ever seen one?"

"No, son, I haven't. They live deep in the woods and usually don't come out of their hiding places except at night. But I've seen some of the destruction they've caused. They push their snouts into the ground, trying to find food, and tear up everything in their path. They eat lots of the nuts and berries the bears need to survive the winter. Park rangers try to hunt and trap the boars, but it doesn't do much good."

"Are the boars the reason we saw so many dead trees up on Clingman's Dome today?"

"No, those trees were killed by a tiny insect that has destroyed almost every Fraser fir in the mountains. And that's not the only kind of tree that was lost to something other than logging. Back in the 1920s, a fungus killed every chestnut tree in North America, including the ones in the Smoky Mountains.

"And pollution is damaging the trees, too. The smoke above these mountains isn't just caused by moisture anymore—factories and car exhaust are turning the clean blue smoke into an ugly, smelly gray."

"How many trees did the loggers cut down?"

"Hundreds of thousands of acres. Luckily, the park was established in time to save about 150,000 acres of what is called 'old-growth forest.' The Great Smoky Mountains has the largest stand of virgin timber in the eastern part of the United States."

"How big are the old trees?"

"Some of them are more than a hundred feet tall and so big around that several people could circle one of them and not be able to touch hands. Those trees were already growing before white people ever came to these mountains."

"Are we going to see some of them while we're here?"

"Depends on how far you're willing to hike. The old trees are way up high on the mountain, where it was too tough for the lumber companies to go. But we can take a day and head up the trail above Laurel Falls if you want. . . ."

Brandon's dad didn't finish his sentence. Brandon wasn't listening. He was curled up in his warm sleeping bag, snoring contentedly and dreaming of all the wonderful things he still had left to do on his visit to the Great Smoky Mountains.

BIBLIOGRAPHY

Albright, Rodney and Priscilla Albright. *Hiking Great Smoky Mountains.* edited by Doris Gove. 4th ed. Old Saybrook, Conn.: Globe Pequot Press, 1999.

Cantu, Rita. *Great Smoky Mountains—The Story Behind the Scenery.* Las Vegas: KC Publications, 1989.

Frome, Michael. *Strangers in High Places: The Story of the Great Smoky Mountains.* expanded ed. Knoxville: University of Tennessee Press, 1989.

Manning, Russ, and Sondra Jamieson. *The Best of the Great Smoky Mountains National Park: A Hiker's Guide to Trails and Attractions.* Norris, Tenn.: Mountain Laurel Place, 1991.

Shields, A. Randolph. *The Cades Cove Story.* edited by Paula A. Degen. Gatlinburg, Tenn.: Great Smoky Mountain Natural History Association, 1977.

Chapter Thirteen

RIDE WITH PRIDE
Celebrating the Tennessee Walking Horse

Floodlights illuminate the huge outdoor arena in Shelbyville, Tennessee. The 30,000 people gathered there are eating and drinking and talking and laughing.

A voice booms over the loudspeaker. "Ladies and gentlemen, the event you've all been waiting for is about to begin. Welcome to the Championship Class of the Tennessee Walking Horse Celebration!"

The crowd cheers. An organ begins playing "The Tennessee Waltz." All eyes turn toward the gate that opens onto the track.

Suddenly the horses appear, one right after another, walking in perfect rhythm to the beat of the music. Their coats glisten and their long, full tails are arched proudly. Brightly colored ribbons are woven into their braided manes.

The riders, dressed in starched shirts, tailored riding coats, and shiny jodhpur boots, sit nearly motionless in their saddles as the horses glide around the track once, twice, three times.

"Riders, go running walk," the announcer says as the organ music grows livelier.

The horses move more quickly now. They lift their front feet high into the air and nod their heads in rhythm to the music. Their coats are shiny with sweat. The crowd is standing, shouting and cheering and whistling.

One of the horses circling the ring in front of them will be crowned the World Grand Champion—the greatest honor a Tennessee Walking Horse can receive.

A plantation pleasure Tennessee Walking Horse (Courtesy TWHBEA)

The story of the Tennessee Walking Horse begins more than 200 years ago, when pioneers crossed the Appalachian Mountains from Virginia and North Carolina into what would become the state of Tennessee. These early settlers brought many different kinds—or *breeds*—of horses with them.

Some of the horses could run very fast. Some were sturdy enough to pull a plow or haul a heavy wagon. Some were comfortable enough to ride all day long. And some of them were extraordinarily beautiful and had quiet, gentle personalities.

But there was not one breed of horse that had *all* of those characteristics.

People who raised horses soon came up with an idea to change that.

"If I breed my fast stallion to your sturdy mare," one farmer said to his neighbor, "we might get a foal that's fast *and* sturdy."

"And if I breed my gentle mare to your smooth-riding stallion, we might get a foal that's gentle *and* smooth," said another.

"And when those foals grow up, we can breed them to each other. Sooner or later, maybe we'll come up with a whole new kind of horse," the farmers said, "a horse that's fast and sturdy, and smooth and gentle!"

That's just what happened. Beginning in the mid 1800s, horse owners began to mate four different breeds of horses—Morgans, Thoroughbreds, American Saddle Horses, and Standardbreds. The owners kept records of the foals that were born and of what kind of horse each foal was bred to when it grew up.

As the years passed, a new breed did evolve. At first, it was called a *Plantation Horse*, because it was so comfortable to ride that a plantation owner could spend hours in the saddle and not be sore or tired at the end of the day.

The Plantation Horse had all the good characteristics that breeders had hoped for. But one characteristic stood out above all the rest. What made this new horse special was its gaits.

A *gait* is the way a horse moves its feet. All breeds have a slow gait called a walk. When a horse walks, each of its four feet hits the ground separately. In most breeds, the hoof prints made by the back feet will fall alongside or a little behind the hoof prints made by the front feet.

The Plantation Horse made a different hoof print. Its rear feet glided beyond the prints made by the front feet—right rear over right front and left rear over left front. This is known as *overstride*. No other breed of horse walks that way naturally.

Because of its unique walk, Plantation Horses soon came to be called Tennessee Walking Horses.

Unlike most other horses, Tennessee Walking Horses do not trot. Instead, they have a gait known as the *running walk*. The running walk is simply a faster walk. Walking Horses can travel up to twenty miles-per-hour at this gait and sometimes achieve an overstride of eighteen inches. The more overstride a horse has, the better a "walker" it is considered to be.

The running walk is the gait that made Tennessee Walking Horses famous. As the horse pulls with its forelegs and drives forward with its hindquarters, it nods its head in rhythm with the movement of its feet. Some Walkers even flop their ears and snap their teeth in sync with their running walk!

The three gaits of the Tennessee Walking Horse (Courtesy TWHBEA)

The third gait is the *canter*—a slow, easy gallop. As a horse canters, one of its front feet hits the ground alone. Then the other front foot and the opposite back foot hit the ground together. Finally, the remaining back foot hits the ground. Most breeds canter, but the Tennessee Walking Horse's canter is so gentle and soothing that it has been nicknamed the "rocking chair gait."

Walking Horses do not have to be taught these special gaits—they just come naturally. Even a newborn foal frolicking beside its mother moves in the distinctive ways that only Tennessee Walking Horses can.

"My horse is so smooth, I can ride from sunup to sundown without getting tired," one owner would brag to another.

"My children can carry baskets full of eggs to market without cracking a single one," another would boast.

"My wife straps our baby to the saddle while she rides. That young'n naps for hours without a peep!" a third one would add.

For many years, there was no organization that kept track of ownership and pedigrees of Walking Horses. In 1935 an organization known as the Tennessee Walking Horse Breeders' and Exhibitors' Association was formed in Lewisburg, Tennessee. Its purpose is to keep records and to let the American people know what a wonderful animal the Tennessee Walking Horse is.

In 1950, more than 100 years after the earliest Walking Horses were born, the U.S. Department of Agriculture officially recognized the Tennessee Walking Horse as a distinct breed.

Allan, Merry Go Boy, and Midnight Sun are three of the most famous Walking Horses in history. Descendents of these horses are still winning shows and being sold for many thousands of dollars.

Long before there was an "official" Tennessee Walking Horse, there were Walking Horse shows. Anywhere there was even a handful of Walking Horse owners, there was likely to be a show.

Walking Horses were shown in county fairs and at Independence Day pageants. Farmers often worked their horses in the fields all day and then rode them into town in the evening to compete with other Walking Horses. The dirt road around a courthouse square was usually the show ring. Instead of trophies, ribbons, or money, the prizes in those early shows were often groceries or animal feed.

In the spring of 1939, Henry Davis had an idea for a much grander Walking Horse show than had ever been held before. He began to talk to some of the civic clubs in Shelbyville, Tennessee.

"I've just come from the Crimson Clover Festival in Winchester," he told them. "And my wife's recently been to a blueberry festival up north. Those festivals bring lots of fame and money to the towns that host them."

"What does that have to do with Shelbyville?" some of the club members asked.

"We have an asset that's a whole lot more interesting than blueberries or clover," Davis answered. "We have Tennessee Walking Horses!"

Davis persuaded several clubs to provide tickets, programs, and food for a Walking Horse festival. In September 1939, the first Tennessee Walking Horse Celebration was held at the high school football field in Shelbyville. The 8,000 spectators who attended watched as a horse named Strolling Jim became the first World Grand Champion.

The Celebration has been held every year since 1939, but it has seen lots of changes. It has grown to be the biggest horse show in the world, attracting hundreds of competitors and thousands of spectators from across the country and around the world.

The show lasts ten days now instead of four, beginning the last week in August and ending on the Saturday night before Labor Day. The main events are held in a huge outdoor stadium that seats

30,000 people. The stadium is surrounded by a 100-acre equestrian complex which includes an indoor arena and luxurious horse barns and practice areas.

More than half a million dollars in prize money is awarded every year to competitors at the Celebration. A horse that might have been worth only a few thousand dollars before the show is likely to be worth many times that after winning a big prize. Many of the World Grand Champion horses were later sold for hundreds of thousands of dollars. Some of them have brought more than a million dollars!

Crowds come to the Celebration to watch the finest Tennessee Walking Horses in the world performing in all kinds of contests.

Some of the horses compete in cowboy events, racing around barrels or weaving their way through a series of plastic poles stuck into the ground.

Some of them jump hedges and fences.

Some dash around a track, pulling a carriage.

Others compete in contests that show just how smoothly a Walking Horse moves. One of these events is the egg-and-spoon contest, where riders balance a raw egg in a teaspoon while the horses circle the track. The rider whose egg is the last to fall off the spoon is the winner.

Another contest, the water glass race, began at a county fair in the early 1930s. A rider held a glass full of water on the palm of his hand while his horse performed a high-speed running walk. Not a single drop of water spilled. Ever since then, water glass races have been popular events at most Walking Horse shows.

But the reason most spectators come to the Celebration is to watch high-dollar horses perform the distinctive *Big Lick* running walk.

The word *lick* refers to the way a Walking Horse lifts its front feet. Not long after the first Celebration was held, competitors began to notice that the faster a horse performed the running walk and the higher he stepped, the more the crowd cheered. The bigger a horse's lick was, the more likely he was to win a prize.

Although Walking Horses can be trained to do the Big Lick naturally, trainers soon came up with ways to speed the process along. They put thick leather pads and heavy shoes on the horses' front

Competitors in a water glass race (Courtesy TWHBEA)

feet. Many trainers also added chains to the horses' front legs. The increased height and weight were not painful to the horses, and it made them step higher than they ever had before.

Some unscrupulous owners and trainers resorted to *soring* their horses' front legs. They burned them with chemicals or injected irritating liquids under their skin. When sored horses' feet hit the ground, the pain made them lift their legs extremely high.

There was a huge public outcry when people learned about such cruel practices. Although most owners and trainers of Tennessee Walking Horses did not sore their horses or mistreat them in any way, the few that did brought embarrassment to everyone associated with Walking Horses. Some people predicted that if the shameful practice of soring was not stopped, it would mean death to the Walking Horse industry.

In 1957, the Tennessee General Assembly passed a law making it illegal to sore a horse. In 1970, the U.S. Congress made it a federal crime. The laws require a team of officials to check every Walking Horse each time it is shown, to make sure that nothing inhumane has been done to it. Owners and trainers who are found guilty of abusing horses are fined and sometimes imprisoned. In severe cases, violators can be disqualified from ever showing horses again.

As the years have passed, Tennessee Walking Horses have become more and more famous and popular. In fact, their popularity is growing faster than any other breed in the United States. More than 400,000 Walking Horses are registered with the TWHBEA.

And those horses aren't found just in Tennessee. They are raised in most of the fifty states and in several foreign countries, including Canada, Germany, and Australia.

What are people doing with all those Tennessee Walking Horses? Some of them are competing in horse shows, but most are not. Many people who own Walking Horses use them simply for pleasure riding.

Walking Horse owners compare the ride of their horses to that of the finest luxury car in the world. They talk of how intelligent and easy to train their horses are.

They remind listeners that all of Roy Rogers's trails were happy because Trigger was a Tennessee Walking Horse.

Most of them claim they wouldn't swap one Tennessee Walking Horse for a dozen horses of any other breed. Who can blame them?

BIBLIOGRAPHY

A Look At 50 Years of Celebrating, 1939-1988 (video). Tennessee Walking Horse National Celebration, Shelbyville, Tenn.

Tennessee Walking Horse Breeders' and Exhibitors' Association Youth Handbook. Lewisburg, Tenn.

Webb, Joe. *The Care and Training of the Tennessee Walking Horse.* Lamar, Ark.: by the author.

Womack, Bob. *The Echo of Hoofbeats: The History of the Tennessee Walking Horse.* Shelbyville, Tenn.: Dabora Inc., 1984.

Chapter Fourteen

CITY WITH A SECRET
Oak Ridge Builds the Bomb

The old man's name was John Hendrix. His hair and beard were long and white, and he had a wild look in his eyes. Lots of folks thought he was crazy. Some even said so.

Hendrix was a deeply religious man who loved to spend time meditating in the woods near his East Tennessee home. One winter day in 1900, a voice as loud as thunder spoke to him from the sky.

"Go alone into the mountains to pray," the voice said. "You will be shown visions of what the future holds for this land."

Hendrix obeyed. He went deep into the forest, laid his head upon a rock, and stayed forty days and forty nights. Legend says that it was so cold that Hendrix's hair froze to the ground. While he was lying there he did see a startling vision. He knew he must return home and tell his neighbors about it.

"I've seen it coming," he told them. "Bear Creek valley will change. There will be a city on Black Oak Ridge. Big engines will dig big ditches. There will be noise and confusion, and the earth will shake. Thousands of people will run to and fro. This valley will someday fill with great buildings and factories, and they will help win the greatest war that will ever be.

"I've seen it. It's coming. . . ."

John Hendrix died not long after telling of his vision. People soon forgot about his prophecy. The area where Hendrix had lived remained rural and peaceful, disconnected in many ways from the outside world.

But events in Europe in the late 1930s were to change all that. East Tennessee, like most other places in the world, would feel the effects of these events.

In 1939, Adolf Hitler—the leader of Nazi Germany—ordered his army to invade Poland. World War II began. It was to become the largest and most terrible war humankind had ever witnessed.

There were many brilliant scientists living in Germany during the 1930s. Because they feared Hitler, several of them left their homeland and immigrated to the United States. Albert Einstein was one of those scientists.

He and others knew that important scientific experiments were taking place in Germany. Chemists and physicists were studying atomic fission. They had discovered that it was possible to split atoms of uranium, thus releasing tremendous amounts of energy. Such energy, if put into a bomb, would have unimaginable powers of destruction. The first nation to make such a weapon would have a huge advantage in the war.

Einstein thought it was important to warn President Franklin Roosevelt about what German scientists were doing, so he wrote the President a letter.

"Sir," the letter said. "Some recent work leads me to expect that the element uranium may be turned into a new and important source of energy in the near future. It may be possible to set up a nuclear chain reaction . . . which would lead to the construction of bombs."

Einstein urged that American scientists become involved right away in nuclear research. It was vital to the safety of the Free World that the United States develop an atomic bomb before Hitler did.

At first, President Roosevelt did not pay much attention to what Einstein and his colleagues were saying. He had other, more important worries. But when the United States entered World War II in 1941 after the Japanese attack on Pearl Harbor, Roosevelt suddenly became very interested in research on atomic bombs.

He appointed a team of scientists and government administrators to find an area where such research could take place. Brigadier General Leslie Groves of the U.S. Army Corps of Engineers was put in charge.

"We need to find a place far enough from the coast that it won't be open to enemy attack," Groves told his team.

"It must have plenty of water and an abundant source of electricity. And we need to choose a spot that's sparsely populated, since we'll have to move all the people off of it."

In the fall of 1942, dozens of surveyors descended on Anderson and Roane counties, in East Tennessee. An area near the Clinch River, just a few miles northwest of Knoxville, seemed to be the perfect spot to build a city dedicated to atomic research.

But before that city could be built, the 1,000 families who lived in the tiny farming communities of Elza, Robertsville, Scarboro, and Wheat would have to be removed.

Some of those people came home after a day working in the fields to find a flimsy paper note tacked to a gatepost. Others were greeted by a polite but insistent knock on their front doors. They all received the same message:

THE WAR DEPARTMENT INTENDS TO TAKE POSSESSION OF YOUR FARM. IT WILL BE NECESSARY FOR YOU TO MOVE. YOUR FULLEST COOPERATION WILL BE A MATERIAL AID TO THE WAR EFFORT.

Most people didn't know how to react. Some families had occupied the same piece of land for several generations. Some had moved to the area in the 1920s and 1930s after the government had bought other land they owned.

One mountain man had reluctantly sold the land where he was born to the National Park Service in 1928 so that the Great Smoky Mountains National Park could be created. He'd been forced to sell again a few years later when his new land was needed for the construction of Norris Dam. Now it was 1942 and the government was asking him for the third time to sell his property.

"If I knew a place where there weren't no government men to dodge, I'd shore go there!" he said.

Almost all the farmers who were asked to sell their land had crops in the fields waiting to be harvested. Their barns were filled with hay, and their houses were filled with furniture. Most of them did not own a car or truck. How could they possibly move their families and possessions in the short amount of time the government had allowed?

The residents complained about having to move. They didn't want to leave crops and farm animals behind. Many felt they were not being offered enough money for their property. They worried about finding a new place to live.

But in the end, all but a few of them moved away.

"What can you do?" one Scarboro resident remarked. "The government needs your land to win the war. Who could refuse such a request as that?"

Another man commented that he had three sons in the service—two of them overseas. "I figured that if giving up my home and my land would help bring them home sooner, I'd be happy to do it," he said.

Just a few weeks after the farms were vacated, thousands of engineers, scientists, and construction workers swarmed onto the newly purchased 59,000 acres in East Tennessee. Their goal was to design and build three huge facilities, where researchers would try different methods of splitting the atom.

They had another goal, too—they had to keep the project a secret from everyone, including even those who were working there. The U.S. government had a code name for the development of the atomic bomb—"The Manhattan Project."

The new town was first called Clinton Engineering Works, named after nearby Clinton, Tennessee. Construction workers had a better idea. Because the town was located near a high cliff known as "Black Oak Ridge," the workers suggested calling it "Oak Ridge."

The name stuck.

John Hendrix's prophecy was coming true. Hundreds of machines with big engines came into the valley. Those machines dug big ditches. There was noise and confusion, and the earth shook. Thousands of people ran to and fro. Within a few months, the once-quiet area was filled with great buildings and factories, designed to help win the greatest war that had ever been fought.

And around it all was a fence. Because Oak Ridge had a secret.

Some of the most brilliant scientific minds in the United States were working with a single purpose: to produce weapons-grade enriched uranium that could be used to fuel the most powerful bomb the world had ever known.

Aerial view of the K-25 plant during early construction
(Photo by James Edward Wescott, courtesy of U.S. Department of Energy
Collection, Oak Ridge Room, ORPL)

Three huge plants—giant windowless buildings with the names K-25, Y-12, and X-10—were constructed in just a few months. They were in operation twenty-four hours a day, seven days a week.

K-25, a mile-and-a-half long U-shaped building, covered 1,500 acres—more than any building ever constructed in history. It was so enormous that employees often rode bicycles to get from one part of the factory to the others. Workers in this plant experimented with the gaseous diffusion method of uranium separation.

Y-12 was located in the southern part of town. Scientists there studied electromagnetic separation of uranium.

Experiments at X-10, today known as the Oak Ridge National Laboratory, focused on methods of converting uranium into plutonium.

The people who planned Oak Ridge thought that about 12,000 workers would be needed to operate the atomic research facilities and to run the town. They were wrong.

As research on the bomb progressed, more and more workers were needed. Along with plant employees came construction workers, teachers, plumbers, shopkeepers, barbers, electricians, doctors, dentists, clerical workers, waitresses, custodians, and people who performed dozens of other jobs.

By the summer of 1945—less than three years after the huge digging machines first came to Bear Creek valley—more than 75,000 people lived and worked in Oak Ridge. It had become the fifth-largest city in Tennessee.

But only one percent of Oak Ridgers knew what was *really* going on there.

Tennessee governor Prentice Cooper didn't know. Members of Congress didn't know. It was even said that Harry Truman—then the Vice President of the United States—didn't know what kind of work was being done in Oak Ridge.

One man described his job this way: "I didn't know what or why I was doing what I did, only that it was my job. Whether we turned valves, typed in an office, or helped put the big puzzle together, we were dumb as to what we were doing."

"We were working on something to end the war," a woman explained. "We didn't know what it was."

"It was not considered proper to discuss what anyone did for a living," another said. "Everything was a secret. We knew it was for the war—that was enough!"

Of course, top-level scientists and government officials knew exactly what was going on. But they also knew how vitally important it was not to reveal the secret to anyone.

Billboards, posters, and signs on buses constantly reminded Oak Ridgers to remain quiet about their work. BE SMART! PLAY DUMB! KEEP MUM! one poster said. Another stated, LOOSE LIPS SINK SHIPS!

Another showed the famous picture of three monkeys, one covering its eyes, the second its ears, while the third covered its mouth. WHAT YOU SEE HERE, WHAT YOU DO HERE, WHAT YOU HEAR HERE, WHEN YOU LEAVE HERE,

This Oak Ridge billboard stresses security. (Photos by Wescott, courtesy of ORPL)

These Oak Ridge billboards stress security.
(Photos by Wescott, courtesy of ORPL)

LET IT STAY HERE, it warned. Fear of foreign spies and enemy agents kept security tight. Every person who applied for any kind of employment in Oak Ridge was interviewed, photographed, fingerprinted, and put through a background check before being hired.

Oak Ridge was ten miles long and two miles wide. A high chain-link fence, topped with barbed wire and patrolled by guards on horseback, surrounded the entire city. Uniformed soldiers with machine guns maintained a constant watch at the seven gates that were the only passageways into or out of Oak Ridge. Everyone over the age of twelve was required to wear an ID badge at all times.

Mail was inspected. Telephones were tapped. Binoculars, cameras, and telescopes had to be registered with Army authorities. Lie detector tests were administered to everyone who worked in the nuclear plants.

Oak Ridge wasn't on any map, and no road signs gave directions to the secret city.

"Where are you?" one mother wrote to her son. "I can't find anybody in the whole state of Tennessee who has any idea where Oak Ridge is."

One grocer complained to his supplier that a load of merchandise he had ordered several weeks earlier still hadn't arrived. The supplier wrote back and said he couldn't ship anything to Oak Ridge. No one could tell him where it was, so he didn't believe there was such a place.

Military police check vehicles entering Oak Ridge.
(Photo by Wescott, courtesy ORPL)

Fanciful stories about what was being manufactured in Oak Ridge circulated constantly among the town's children. Some of them claimed the plants were making paper dolls or butterfly wings. Others insisted that it was playing cards or suitcases for President Roosevelt's wife, Eleanor.

One man told his young daughter, "If anybody asks you what I make, just tell them it's holes for doughnuts and lights for lightning bugs."

Adults had some crazy theories, too, though they were more reluctant to voice them. Were the giant plants producing rockets that could reach the moon? Perhaps they were inventing miracle drugs. Or maybe they were making campaign buttons for the next time Franklin Roosevelt ran for President.

Most people probably suspected that their town was involved in some kind of weapons research, but nobody said that out loud.

There was a war on and the enemy might have been listening.

Secrecy was a way of life in Oak Ridge. Well-known scientists used fictitious names. Many of the most important people in town were not listed in the phone book. Girl Scouts registered by first

Brownie troop at Elm Grove School in Oak Ridge
(Photo by Wescott, courtesy ORPL)

name only. Newspaper accounts of high school sports contests listed none of the players' last names.

There was a war on and the enemy might have been listening.

From outside the gates, Oak Ridge looked like an Army post. From the inside, it looked like a mess.

Bulldozers and backhoes had destroyed once-beautiful fields and forests. There was no escaping the mud and dust. Few of the roads were paved or graveled. Most were just plain dirt. There were no curbs or gutters. Wooden sidewalks called "boardwalks" wove willy-nilly through the town.

Oak Ridgers claimed that their town was the only place on earth where a person could stand in mud up to his neck and have dust blow in his face.

Residents quickly learned to wear galoshes wherever they went and to carry their "good shoes" in a sack. One man recalled the time his date for a formal dance greeted him at the door wearing a lovely ball gown and rubber wading boots!

"I thought it was the ugliest city in the world," one woman said

Mrs. Wilson J. Schreck outside her trailer home, 1944
(Photo by Wescott, courtesy ORPL)

about her first sight of Oak Ridge. "It was nothing but a sea of red mud. It was horribly hot and noisy. The sound of machinery drowned out the birds' songs. There weren't many cars, but there were lots of buses, all painted olive green with camouflage on top. I wondered if I had been sent to live in a prison."

Housing in Oak Ridge was of minor importance to the city planners. The nuclear plants were what really mattered, but workers had to have someplace to live.

Some of them stayed in trailers. Many lived in drab dormitories or apartments. African-American workers were assigned the most dismal housing of all. They lived in *hutments*—tiny, windowless plywood buildings with dirt floors and no furnishings other than sleeping cots and a potbellied stove.

The most privileged workers—usually scientists, managers, and families with children—lived in *victory cottages,* or *cemestos.* These houses were precut and boxed and were delivered in sections on flatbed trucks. The houses came ready for occupancy—complete with appliances, furniture, and even window curtains!

Builders could assemble hundreds of the small, simple houses at a time. During the peak of construction, a house went up every thirty minutes. Stores, playgrounds, and recreation centers soon sprang up throughout town. Schools did, too.

Because everyone in Oak Ridge had come from somewhere else, emotional bonds among students developed quickly. "There was no such thing as a new kid in town," one woman explained. "We were all new kids, and that made it easier to be friends."

Another person remembered the diversity in Oak Ridge High School's first graduating class. "We had students from all forty-eight states and several foreign countries. Getting to know those people . . . exchanging ideas and viewpoints with them . . . teasing each other about our accents . . . was as much an education as anything I learned from textbooks."

Along with schools, other educational and cultural institutions were soon established in Oak Ridge. Churches were built. A chorus, a concert band, and a symphony provided music for the town. A library and a community theater began. Clubs that catered to many different interests, from horseback riding to growing African violets, were organized.

There was also a demand for sports facilities. A miniature golf course, skating rink, bowling alley, swimming pool, and tennis courts were soon built.

And because the nuclear plants operated twenty-four hours a day, most of the recreational facilities did, too.

"It was never dark in Oak Ridge," one man recalled. "As soon as the sun went down, the big streetlights came on. They blazed until morning. You could eat, bowl, or go to a movie whenever you wanted. We lived in a city that didn't sleep."

Throughout the war years, many products that the armed forces needed were in short supply for civilians. Such food items as meat, sugar, eggs, and coffee were rationed. It was often difficult to buy gasoline or rubber tires because they were needed for military vehicles. Even soap and cigarettes were hard to come by.

Standing in line to purchase rationed items became a way of life in Oak Ridge, just as it did in most parts of the United States.

"My parents made sure I always had extra money in case I saw a line at the drugstore or the grocery," one woman recalled. "Sometimes the storekeeper ran out of whatever it was before my turn came, but that's the chance we took. That was an understood rule during the war years—if you see a line, get in it."

People in Oak Ridge often joked that their giant factories really weren't making anything at all. "Truckloads of materials come into the city," they said. "But nothing ever goes out."

That wasn't exactly true. For three years the nuclear research facilities had been extracting small amounts of enriched uranium, or U-235, from tons of raw uranium ore.

In March 1945, the first shipments of enriched uranium left Oak Ridge for a plant in Los Alamos, New Mexico. That was where the actual atomic bomb was being designed and built. By July, Oak Ridge had supplied Los Alamos with about thirty pounds of U-235.

The bomb was successfully tested on a flat, uninhabited desert in New Mexico at dawn on July 16, 1945. Its energy, four times hotter than the sun, created a huge explosion and a giant mushroom-shaped cloud.

The atomic age had arrived.

Franklin Roosevelt had died in April. Harry Truman was now President of the United States. When he learned of the awesome power of the atomic bomb, he decided that dropping it on Japan would be the quickest and best way to bring World War II to an end.

In late July the United States and its allies called for Japan's unconditional surrender. They warned that refusal would result in massive destruction. The Japanese government ignored the warning.

On August 6, 1945, a bomb nicknamed "Little Boy" and fueled by U-235 produced in Oak Ridge was loaded onto the airplane *Enola Gay*. The bomb was ten feet long and weighed 9,000 pounds. It had the explosive power of 20,000 tons of dynamite.

At 8:15 A.M. Little Boy was dropped on the Japanese city of Hiroshima.

Seventy thousand people were killed. At least that many more were wounded. The city itself was completely wiped out. Three days later another atomic bomb, this one nicknamed "Fat Man" and powered by plutonium, exploded over Nagasaki, Japan. Thousands more were killed or wounded.

On August 14 the Empire of Japan surrendered. World War II was over.

Oak Ridge residents celebrate the end of World War II.
(Photo by Wescott, ORPL)

"It's a bomb!" Oak Ridgers exclaimed after hearing the news. "We've been making an atom bomb!"

Reporters and photographers swarmed into Oak Ridge. STORY OF SECRET CITY OFFICIALLY TOLD one headline proclaimed. POWER OF OAK RIDGE ATOMIC BOMB HITS JAPAN and TRUMAN REVEALS USE OF WORLD'S GREATEST BOMB others said.

The people of Oak Ridge were thrilled that the war was over. And they were thrilled at the part their city had played in bringing about Japan's surrender.

There were parades in the streets. Flags waved. Horns honked. Children beat on dishpans with spoons. People danced until dawn. Scientists shouted the word they had long been forbidden to say— "Uranium!"

Out of the Tennessee hills—from a secret city behind a fence— came the weapon which helped win the greatest war that had ever been fought.

Old John Hendrix's vision had become reality.

BIBLIOGRAPHY

Blow, Michael. *The History of the Atomic Bomb*. New York: American Heritage Publishing, 1968.

Gailer, Joanne Stern. *Oak Ridge and Me*. Children's Museum of Oak Ridge, 1991.

Jefferson, Jon. "Swords to Plowshares—A Short History of Oak Ridge National Laboratory." Oak Ridge National Laboratory, 1993.

Johnson, Charles W. and Charles O. Jackson. *City Behind A Fence*. Knoxville: University of Tennessee Press, 1981.

Maienschien, Joyce C. and Eileen A. Neiler. *And the Fence Came Down*. Oak Ridge: Oak Ridge Community Foundation, 1993.

Oak Ridge National Laboratory Review (Vol. 25, nos. 3 and 4).

Overholt, James, ed. *These Are Our Voices: The Story of Oak Ridge, 1942-1970*. Oak Ridge: Children's Museum of Oak Ridge, 1987.

Robinson, George O. *The Oak Ridge Story*. Southern Publishers, Inc., 1950.

Searcy, Jay. "The Secret City," *The Knoxville News-Sentinel*, September 27, 1992.

Chapter Fifteen

I AM A MAN

Black Tennesseans Seek the Promised Land

"Let's get going, Doc!"

It was suppertime on April 4, 1968, and Dr. Martin Luther King, Jr. was running late. He was scheduled to speak at a dinner that evening. As he stepped onto the balcony outside his second-floor room at the Lorraine Motel in Memphis, friends in the parking lot below urged him to hurry.

King smiled to himself. It seemed like they weren't ever going to allow him to slow down. He leaned over the railing to tease them.

The Lorraine Motel, Memphis
(Courtesy University of Memphis special collections)

"I'm coming, I'm coming. Just give me a minute to get my coat."

Suddenly, a single rifle shot rang out. King collapsed onto the concrete floor of the balcony. A bullet had ripped into his face. Blood poured from a hole in his neck. People began crying and screaming. The sounds of sirens were everywhere.

An ambulance rushed King to St. Joseph's Hospital, where doctors discovered that his jugular vein was torn and his spinal cord severed. They could not save his life. King died at 7:05 P.M. He was thirty-nine years old.

Martin Luther King, Jr. had come to Memphis to support African-American sanitation workers who were on strike. The workers had walked off their jobs to protest the low pay and horrible conditions under which many of them labored.

The strikers carried signs with the words I AM A MAN on them.

They had chosen that slogan for a couple of reasons. Some white people called adult black men "boy" as a way to make them feel inferior. African-Americans wanted that to change.

The garbage workers also chose the slogan because they felt that they were not treated as first-class human beings at their jobs. White workers were paid better wages and often allowed to work more hours each week. Almost half of the African-American sanitation workers were paid so little that they had to rely on welfare to feed their families. They received no health care benefits, retirement pensions, or vacations.

Though the sanitation workers spent long hours each day handling smelly, leaking garbage cans, Memphis city officials did not even provide a place for them to shower or to eat when their workday was finished.

During bad weather, white garbage collectors were allowed to seek shelter inside buildings. African-American garbage collectors were not. A few weeks before the strike began, two black workers had climbed inside a garbage truck to try to stay dry during a thunderstorm. They had been crushed to death when the compacting mechanism was accidentally turned on.

The sanitation workers hoped that if King became involved in

Striking Memphis Sanitation Workers
(Courtesy University of Memphis special collections)

their cause, city officials might be persuaded to treat African-Americans fairly. At first King refused to come to Memphis. He was busy planning a "Poor People's March" to Washington, D.C., which he hoped would make lawmakers and the public more aware of injustice and discrimination throughout the country.

Martin Luther King, Jr. had spent most of his adult life working to bring about racial equality. *Jim Crow* laws forced black people and white people to stay apart in almost all aspects of life—in schools, movie theaters, restaurants, on public transportation, and even in rest rooms and at drinking fountains.

African-Americans were not allowed to enter places where there were signs that said WHITES ONLY. And there were lots of those signs all over the South.

King believed that the best way to deal with hatred and injustice was through passive resistance. He had studied the words and actions of Jesus Christ and Mahatma Gandhi, and he believed that the lessons those two had taught were the right way to bring about change.

"You have heard that it was said, An eye for an eye and a tooth for a tooth," Jesus says in the New Testament, "But I say to you, if anyone strikes you on the right cheek, turn to him the other also.

"You have heard that it was said You shall love your neighbor, and hate your enemy. But I say to you, Love your enemies, and pray for those who persecute you."

Gandhi was a spiritual leader in India who lived almost 2,000 years after Jesus lived. His teachings were very much like Jesus' teachings.

"Never use violence," Gandhi said. "Violence only defeats itself. It only brings about more hate and more violence. Meet body force with soul force. Meet hate with love. Those who want to win their freedom must learn to suffer."

Martin Luther King knew that such advice would oftentimes be hard to follow, but he believed that it was the only right way to behave.

One of King's first acts in his fight for civil rights took place in the 1950s in Montgomery, Alabama. He organized a yearlong bus boycott that ended legal segregation in Montgomery's public transportation system.

He fought hatred and bigotry in Mississippi, Florida, and in his home state of Georgia. He was put in jail many times for disobeying segregation laws.

King had also been to Tennessee to help bring about racial justice. Although Tennessee was more willing than some of the other Southern states to accept the idea of desegregation, things did not always go smoothly.

In 1956, federal courts ordered the all-white Clinton High School in Anderson County to integrate. Governor Frank Clement called out the National Guard to make sure that black students could safely enter the school.

The school was bombed in October of 1958, but because the bombing happened early on a Sunday morning when the building was empty, no one was hurt. Though the school was destroyed, the bombing actually had a good result. People of both races in Clinton realized that the violence had to stop. When the school was rebuilt, black and white students attended peacefully together.

In Nashville, downtown stores were the targets for integration efforts in the 1950s. Most Nashville merchants were happy for black customers to spend money in their stores, but they would not allow them to eat in the store restaurants or snack bars or to use the rest rooms or drink from the water fountains.

Students at the black colleges in Nashville decided that the best way to protest segregation was to stage sit-ins. The students were led by James Lawson, the first African-American to attend Vanderbilt University Divinity School, and by Rev. Kelly Miller Smith, pastor of Capitol Hill First Baptist Church in Nashville.

Like Martin Luther King, Jr., Lawson had studied the teachings of Jesus and Gandhi. He believed that nonviolent passive resistance was the best way to bring about long-lasting change. He spoke in a voice that was low and soothing; sometimes the students had to strain to hear what he way saying.

"Here's what you must do," Lawson told the students. "Go in groups to the restaurants which are refusing you service. Take a seat and act as though you expect to be served."

"But what if we are ignored?" one of the students asked.

"Continue to sit there. Be polite and friendly at all times. Sit straight and face the counter. Don't laugh or act rowdy in any way."

"How long must we sit there?" another student asked.

"Until you are served, or until your group leader gives you permission to leave. Sooner or later, I think you will be waited on, even if the store owners don't like it. You are taking up seats where white customers might want to sit and eat, and that is costing the merchants money."

On February 13, 1960, more than 100 young people, almost all of them black, marched through deep snow from Capitol Hill Baptist Church to downtown Nashville. When white people in the crowd shoved them or shouted obscenities, they did not shove back or shout obscenities in return. They walked on, heads held high.

The students did what Lawson had told them to do. They made purchases at three different stores. Then they took their places on the lunch counter stools in those stores and tried to order food. Some of the waitresses simply paid no attention to them. Others said hurtful things. But no one brought them anything to eat or drink.

Within minutes, the restaurant managers at each store put up signs at the entrances to the lunch counters. FOUNTAIN CLOSED IN INTEREST OF PUBLIC SAFETY, the signs read. The students soon gave up and left.

Nashville lunch counter sit-in (Courtesy Metropolitan Archives of Nashville and Davidson County, *Nashville Banner* Collection)

Twice the following week, the students tried again. There were more of them now, and they staged sit-ins at more lunch counters. But still they were not served.

On February 27, more than 400 black students gathered in downtown Nashville. They were determined not to give up on the ideal of racial justice. Hostile crowds of white youths had gathered, too, and they began to abuse the demonstrators. They shouted obscene words at the black students. They spit on them. They hit them and kicked them and burned them with lighted cigarettes.

It was hard for the students to follow their two most important rules, but they did.

Don't strike back or curse if attacked. Remember love and nonviolence.

They took their places on the stools, sitting straight and facing the lunch counter. Soon the police came, but they did not arrest the white youths who were trying to start fights. They charged the black students with disorderly conduct and arrested them.

As soon as the police hauled one group off to jail, another group of students took their places on the counter stools. Hundreds of demonstrators were waiting in the basement of Kelly Miller Smith's church, willing to take their turns on the stools and in jail. After eighty-one students were arrested and taken to jail, the stores closed down.

It was clear that the sit-ins alone were not going to bring about change. It was time to try a new tactic.

Black leaders met and decided to urge their followers to boycott—to refuse to shop at any store that had a segregated lunch counter. Instead of spending their money in those stores, the demonstrators walked up and down the sidewalks in front of the stores, carrying signs of protest.

It was Easter time, a season when merchants often make lots of money selling spring clothes. But that spring, many white people were afraid to come downtown to shop, and since black people were refusing to shop at all, the stores had very few customers.

Some of the black leaders received threats of violence. Early on the morning of April 19, a bomb was thrown at the home of Z. Alexander Looby, a respected Nashville city councilman and civil rights attorney. Although the house was completely destroyed, Looby and his wife survived.

The bombing proved to be more than Nashville's black community could tolerate. By dawn, hundreds of African-Americans began to gather on the grounds of Tennessee State University. Their plan was to march to the courthouse, where they hoped Mayor Ben West would meet them.

It was not to be a march with singing and hand clapping, but a march of silent protest against racial hatred and injustice. Linking arms and walking three abreast, the demonstrators made their way toward the courthouse. As they passed Fisk University, they were joined by hundreds more students. Many of the neighbors watching from their front porches joined, too.

By the time the demonstrators reached the courthouse, their line was ten blocks long. Almost 4,000 people were taking part in the march.

Mayor West met the demonstrators on the courthouse steps. He smiled and made some remarks about leadership.

Then a young black woman, Diane Nash, asked the mayor a question. "Mayor, will you use the prestige of your office to end racial segregation?"

The mayor immediately spoke up. "I appeal to all citizens to end discrimination, to have no hatred or bigotry."

That answer wasn't specific enough for Nash. "Do you mean that to include lunch counters?" she asked.

West took a deep breath. He looked at the sea of black faces stretching before him. His political future, as well as the destiny of his city, was resting on his answer.

"Yes!" West said.

With that one word, Nashville began to change. It became the first Southern city to desegregate public facilities. Martin Luther King, Jr. came to town to celebrate the victory. He spoke to a crowd of thousands of supporters at Fisk University.

"The only thing uncertain about the death of segregation throughout this nation," he said, "is when it will be buried."

The city of Memphis had its troubles, too. Like other cities and towns in Tennessee and throughout the South at the beginning of the 1960s, the Jim Crow tradition ran deep there.

African-Americans could not use the public libraries or enjoy the city parks or the Memphis zoo. They had to sit separately at the back of city buses and were denied service in restaurants just as blacks in Nashville had been.

Although the Civil Rights Act of 1964 said that people of all colors had to be treated equally, that is not usually what happened. People of different races seldom lived in the same neighborhood. Black children often attended schools that were not as good as the schools white children attended. And most African-Americans still worked in the most menial, lowest-paying jobs.

Even when black workers performed the same jobs as white workers, they did not receive the same treatment. That was why the black sanitation workers in Memphis went on strike in February of 1968, and why they asked Martin Luther King, Jr. to come and lend support to their cause.

Even though King was busy, he decided that he couldn't say no to his African-American brothers in Tennessee. He went to Memphis.

Martin Luther King, Jr. made many speeches in his life, but the speech he made on April 3, 1968, is one of his most famous. In that speech, he spoke words that some listeners later said predicted his own death.

King delivers his "Mountaintop" speech.
(Courtesy University of Memphis special collections)

"I've been to the mountaintop," he said. "And I've looked over, and I've seen the promised land. I may not get there with you. But I want you to know tonight that we as a people will get to the promised land. So I'm happy tonight. I'm not worried about anything. I'm not fearing any man. Mine eyes have seen the glory of the coming of the Lord!"

Less than twenty-four hours later, King became the victim of an assassin's bullet.

Two months after he died, an escaped convict named James Earl Ray was arrested for the murder. Prosecutors claimed that Ray had fired the fatal gunshot from a boarding house across the street from the Lorraine Motel. Ray pled guilty and was sentenced to ninety-nine years in prison.

Today the Lorraine Motel in Memphis is the site of the National Civil Rights Museum. The room where King stayed has been preserved to look just as it did on the last day of his life. A wreath hangs on the balcony where he was shot.

The museum is designed to help visitors understand the civil rights movement by experiencing the sights, sounds, and emotions of key events—including lunch counter sit-ins and the Memphis sanitation workers' strike—that helped change the lives of African-Americans in Tennessee and throughout the nation.

BIBLIOGRAPHY

Beifuss, Joan Turner. *At the River I Stand: Memphis, the 1968 Strike, and Martin Luther King*. Brooklyn: Carlson Publishing, 1989.

Lane, Mark. *Murder in Memphis: The FBI and the Assassination of Martin Luther King*. New York: Thunder's Mouth Press, 1993.

McAdory, Jeff. *I Am a Man: Photographs of the 1968 Memphis Sanitation Strike and Dr. Martin Luther King, Jr*. Memphis: Memphis Publishing, 1993.

Peck, Ira. *The Life and Words of Martin Luther King, Jr*. New York: Scholastic, 1968.

Chapter Sixteen

YOU'LL NEVER ESCAPE FROM HERE, JAMES EARL RAY!

A Mountainside Becomes a Prison

The prisoner sat motionless in the backseat of the patrol car, his hands cuffed in front of him. The drive from Memphis to East Tennessee had been a long one, and he wished he could stretch his legs. The curvy mountain roads made his head hurt and his stomach feel queasy, but he didn't dare complain.

It might be a long time before he took another car ride or saw the world outside prison walls. A very long time.

The year was 1968. The prisoner was James Earl Ray. He had just been convicted of the April murder of civil rights leader Martin Luther King, Jr. His sentence? Ninety-nine years behind bars. His destination? Brushy Mountain State Penitentiary—the toughest prison in all of Tennessee.

Ray closed his eyes. He had seen a lot of jails and prisons in his time. He was forty years old, and he had been locked up for almost half his life. But he was not prepared for the sight that greeted him as the patrol car rolled to a stop.

"Wake up, Ray." One of the guards shoved an elbow into his ribs. "You're home."

He rubbed his eyes and squinted out the car window. Brushy Mountain State Penitentiary loomed in front of him. It looked like a huge medieval castle—a fortress of white stone and barbed wire. Encircling it like a horseshoe were the vertical cliffs of Frozen Head Mountain, rising hundreds of feet straight up.

James Earl Ray had a reputation as an escape artist. He had once

James Earl Ray in police custody
(Photo by Jack Gunter, courtesy Metropolitan Archives of Nashville and
Davidson County, *Nashville Banner* Collection)

boasted to a lawyer that no penitentiary could keep him in. But in the fading sunlight of that late summer afternoon, he wondered if his bragging rights were over. Even if a man could get past those prison walls, scaling that mountain would likely prove impossible.

"Oh, no," he whispered to himself. "How will I ever escape from here?"

Brushy Mountain State Penitentiary is not the oldest prison in Tennessee. It is not the largest prison in Tennessee. But it is by far the most famous prison in Tennessee.

Tennessee's first penitentiary was built in Nashville in the 1830s. It soon became overcrowded, unsanitary, and filled with disease. That prison was replaced with a new building in the 1850s. But it, too, was soon full.

Lawmakers from East Tennessee believed it was time to build a prison in their part of the state. And they had some good ideas about how the prisoners could be kept busy and make money to pay for their upkeep.

"Let's choose land near a forest, so that prisoners can cut the wood to make lumber for the prison building," one of them said.

"Let's find a spot that's good for farming, too," another said. "That way, prisoners can grow their own food."

"And let's build it in coal country, so that prisoners can mine coal for the state government to use," added a third.

Such a spot was found in the Cumberland Mountains of Morgan County. Thirteen thousand acres of land were purchased as the site for the Brushy Mountain State Penitentiary.

The land was beautiful, but it was also treacherous. The prison was to be built in a valley, with steep cliffs surrounding the building on three sides. The fourth side, where the entrance was to be, would be made secure by a guardhouse and the town of Petros.

Even if an inmate were to make it over the prison walls, he would have no place to go.

The original prison, built in 1896, was an L-shaped structure, four stories high and built entirely of wood. The building was sweltering hot in the summer. During the winter, coal-burning stoves filled the rooms with black smoke and unpleasant odors, but they didn't do much to warm the air.

Some of the inmates at Brushy Mountain worked on the prison farm. Others worked in the hospital or the laundry or the kitchen. But most of the prisoners worked in the coal mine.

Prisoners walked out the back door of the building onto a *manway*. This was a 100-foot-long, boxed walkway that led directly into the mineshaft. The manway made it easy for the guards to count the prisoners, and it made it impossible for the prisoners to escape.

The prison soon became so crowded that double use was made of the cells. While half the prisoners worked the mines, the other half occupied the beds in the cellblocks.

At the end of each twelve-hour shift, men with weary muscles and faces caked with black coal dust tromped across the manway and back into the prison, where they took their turns showering, eating, and sleeping. Another group headed across the manway into the mine.

As years went by, the number of inmates at Brushy Mountain

Chapter 10

View of the New Prison, Brushy Mountain, from South East Side.

Brushy Mountain State Prison (Courtesy TSLA)

grew so large that the old building could not hold them all. Construction of a new prison was begun in 1933 and finished two years later. Prisoners did most of the work.

The new building was made of concrete instead of wood. It was designed in the shape of a cross, with two bars of equal length crossing each other at right angles. The prison was three stories high and could hold 630 inmates.

That was the place James Earl Ray was sent after confessing to the assassination of Martin Luther King, Jr. But a few days after he confessed, he began to claim that he was not the killer after all.

"I've been framed," he said. "I didn't do it. I shouldn't have to spend the rest of my life behind bars."

The courts did not believe him, so Ray decided that he would get out of prison another way—by escaping.

He made his first attempt in 1971. His plan was to squeeze through an air vent in his cell and into the prison yard. He would then crawl through a steam tunnel that led to the outside. But the air inside the steam tunnel was nearly 400 degrees, and he was forced to turn back.

He tried to escape again a year later by cutting a hole in the gymnasium roof. That plan failed, too.

But Ray did not give up. "They wouldn't have me in a maximum security prison if I wasn't interested in getting out," he told news reporters. "Sooner or later, I'll find a way to escape."

His next chance came early on the evening of June 11, 1977. Most of the Brushy Mountain inmates were in the exercise yard, closely watched by prison guards. Ray and some other men were playing horseshoes at one end of the yard. Some of the inmates, who knew that Ray planned to escape that night, had promised to start a fight near the basketball court to distract the guards.

They kept their promise, and while the guards were busy breaking up the fight, Ray and six others flung a homemade ladder against the stone wall of the exercise yard. They scrambled up the ladder and under a powerful electric wire strung across the top of the wall.

"Over the wall! Look at the wall!" one of the prisoners in the yard shouted. "James Earl Ray got out!"

Guards reached for their rifles and began firing. They hit one man in the leg and quickly recaptured him. But the rest of the escapees had vanished into the mountain's fog-shrouded forest.

The Brushy Mountain escape whistle sounded six times. That was the signal that let everyone in the prison and in the town of Pet-

Mug shots of James Earl Ray
(Courtesy Tennessee Department of Corrections Public Information Office)

ros know that six inmates were on the loose.

Several police helicopters, more than 150 armed men, and a pack of baying bloodhounds began searching the rugged wilderness. But in the deepening mountain twilight, the escapees had disappeared.

It was only two days later, fifty-five hours after the escape had taken place, that Ray was finally discovered. Cold, dirty, and very hungry, he was huddled under a pile of leaves less than five miles from the prison. He surrendered without a fight.

The "escape-proof penitentiary" had won. That was the last escape attempt for James Earl Ray. He died in 1998 at the age of seventy, never again tasting the freedom he so desperately sought.

Today, Brushy Mountain State Prison looks very much like it has for the past seventy years. It is the oldest operating prison in the state. After the coal ran out, the mine was closed and the manway was removed.

But the concrete structure still sits, huge and sinister, in the face of East Tennessee's rugged cliffs.

The grounds and gardens are tended now by inmates who have shown good behavior and who will soon be released. Parts of the prison are used to house men who are waiting to be sent to other prisons in Tennessee.

In the high-security annex, the most hardened criminals in the state—the worst of the worst—spend their days and nights in solitary confinement. The narrow, barred windows in their cells allow only a tiny glimpse of the outside world. Brushy Mountain State Prison is their home. For some, it is the last home they'll ever know.

And over it, the mountain looms.

BIBLIOGRAPHY

"Brushy Mountain State Prison Tour Guide," (given to visitors at BMSP).

Dickinson, W. Calvin. *Morgan County*. Memphis: Memphis State University Press, 1987.

Goldman, Peter, Tony Fuller, Vern E. Smith, and Elaine Shannon. "Ray's Escape." Newsweek, June 20, 1977.

Winton, Ruth. 1937. A History of Brushy Mountain Penitentiary. Ph. D. diss. University of Tennessee.

Chapter Seventeen

A NEW KIND OF SOUND
Memphis Makes Music

When he was a young boy in Alabama, William Christopher (W. C.) Handy liked to do things most other boys liked to do. He liked to swim. He liked to fish. He liked to play ball and climb trees.

But the thing he most liked to do was to listen.

He listened to the songs of birds. He listened to the chatter of squirrels and the mournful baying of hound dogs. He listened to the long, low whistles of riverboats as they traveled back and forth on the water near his hometown. He listened to black workers singing as they labored in the fields or at the river wharves.

The boy filed every one of those sounds away in his mind. More than anything, he wanted to copy the sounds—to make music of them that he could play over and over again.

W. C. Handy was born in 1873 in a small log cabin in Florence, Alabama, to parents who had been slaves before the Civil War. The family was so poor that they had barely enough money for basic necessities.

W. C. understood at an early age that if he ever wanted to buy something special, he'd have to come up with a way to pay for it himself. What he wanted most in all the world was a guitar. He was sure that if he had one, he could echo the sounds he had been listening to all his life.

So he picked nuts and berries and sold them to his neighbors. He performed odd jobs. He made and sold lye soap. When he finally saved enough money, he went to town and bought a used guitar.

"No!" W. C.'s father said when he saw it. "You'll not bring that instrument of the devil into my house!"

The boy hugged the guitar tightly to him. "But, Papa, I bought it with my own money."

"That makes no difference," his father replied.

"Just listen to the sounds I can make," W. C. said, gently picking the strings.

"Son, music is a sinful pursuit. Your grandfather and I are counting on you to follow in our footsteps and become a minister of the gospel," his father said. "I'd rather see you in the grave than have you become a musician. Now take that guitar back to the store right now."

W. C. did as he was told. He exchanged the guitar for a dictionary. But he never stopped listening to sounds and dreaming of the day he could make his own music.

A schoolteacher taught W. C. the basics of reading and writing music. He taught him to play the cornet. When W. C. was fifteen years old, a Memphis musician came to Florence and organized an orchestra. He persuaded the teenager to join.

W. C. Handy was never the same again.

Defying his parents' wishes, W. C. vowed to make music his life's pursuit. He traveled around the country playing in bands and orchestras. He taught instrumental music and gave voice lessons at the Agricultural and Mechanical College in Alabama.

Everywhere he went, he paid careful attention to what kind of music audiences seemed to like best. W. C. began to combine and polish the songs and sounds he heard. He wrote them down in a new form, using a twelve-bar harmonic structure (in blues and jazz music, the word *bar* is often substituted for the word *measure*, which is a division of time in music) and lyrics that consisted of three-line stanzas (lines of a poem arranged in a rythmic manner).

He had a dream. He wanted to perform his music in Memphis, Tennessee, in one of the most famous musical neighborhoods in the world—a place called Beale Street, located on the banks of the Mississippi River.

Settled by former slaves right after the Civil War, Beale Street had become the center of black civic and social activities in Memphis. There were homes and churches on Beale Street. There were businesses and shops and theaters.

W. C. Handy (Courtesy TSLA)

Most important, at least to W. C. Handy, there were nightclubs where he could play his music.

W. C. moved to Memphis in 1907 and soon became one of the most popular musicians on Beale Street. He had taken music that he had heard all his life—hymns and spirituals that had been sung in his father's church and the songs black people sang as they worked from dawn to dusk—and developed it into a sound that came to be known as "the blues."

W. C. described his music this way: "Each one of my blues is based on some old Negro song of the South . . . something that sticks in my mind, that I hum to myself when I'm not thinking about it . . . some song that is a part of the memories of my childhood and my race."

W. C. lived in Memphis for ten years before moving to New York City. In the 1930s he became blind, but he continued to compose and perform. Before he died in New York in 1958, he had written and published more than forty blues songs.

Some of his most famous are "Memphis Blues," "St. Louis Blues," "Beale Street Blues," "Old Miss Rag," and "Yellow Dog Blues."

After his death, a city block at Beale and Third streets in Memphis was named Handy Park in his memory. It contains a statue of the famous musician holding his beloved cornet.

Although he did not invent the blues, W. C. Handy was the first person to write down that form of music. He made it popular and brought it to a worldwide audience. Because of that, W. C. Handy is known as "The Father of the Blues," and the city of Memphis is known as "The Home of the Blues."

Elvis Presley's birthplace, Tupelo, Mississippi
(Copyright Elvis Presley Enterprises, Inc.)

Memphis has another nickname, too. It's sometimes called "The Birthplace of Rock and Roll."

The most famous rock and roll singer of all time wasn't born in Memphis. He didn't move there until he was thirteen years old. But Elvis Presley—The King of Rock and Roll—considered Memphis his hometown.

In the 1930s a young couple, Vernon and Gladys Presley, lived in Tupelo, Mississippi. Vernon was a truck driver. Gladys worked in a factory as a sewing machine operator.

The Presleys were poor as dirt. Their two-room shack was located in a bad part of town. It had no electricity or running water. In that tiny house on the morning of January 8, 1935, Gladys gave birth to twin boys—Elvis Aaron Presley and his brother Jesse Garon Presley. Jesse was born dead.

Gladys's health was poor and Vernon was frequently out of work. Even as a very young child, Elvis often heard his parents discussing how hard it was to pay the bills.

"Don't you worry none," he told his mother. "When I grow up, I'm going to buy you a fine house and pay everything you owe at the grocery store and get two Cadillacs—one for you and Daddy, and one for me."

The Presleys were a close-knit family. Gladys walked Elvis to and from school every day. "My mama never let me out of her sight if she could help it," Elvis recalled on many occasions.

On Sundays they attended services at a nearby Assembly of God church.

That's where Elvis first came to love music, especially the old-time hymns sung by gospel quartets. One church member recalled that even when Elvis was too little to know the words to songs, he could carry the tunes.

When he was ten years old, Elvis entered a singing contest at a county fair. He sang "Old Shep"—a tearjerking ballad about a boy and his dog. He won second prize—five dollars and a ticket to all the carnival rides. His musical career had begun.

He hoped that on his eleventh birthday his parents would give him a bicycle. They didn't. Bicycles cost too much. But even if they could have afforded one, Gladys was worried that Elvis might get hurt on a bike. She and Vernon gave him a guitar instead.

Elvis was disappointed and angry. "I don't want no part of this thing," he said when he opened the present.

"But, son," Gladys said, "if you'll learn to play this guitar, you might be famous someday."

Little did she know how right she was.

Seeking better jobs, the Presleys moved to Memphis, Tennessee, in 1948. Elvis enrolled in the seventh grade at Humes High School. He was not popular—in fact, most of his classmates considered him strange. His mother still walked him to school. He was skinny and his complexion was bad. And he dressed different than the other students.

Elvis had discovered Beale Street soon after he moved to Memphis. He loved the music and the excitement of the exotic black neighborhood. And he especially loved a clothing store located on Beale Street—Lansky Brothers Department Store.

He began buying most of his clothes—flashy, bizarre outfits, most of them pink and black—at Lansky's. He let his sideburns grow long, and greased his shaggy hair into a pompadour in front and a ducktail in back. He carried his guitar most everywhere he went. It

Beale Street, Memphis (Courtesy TSLA)

was impossible not to notice Elvis Presley.

And Elvis liked it that way.

Elvis graduated from high school in 1953 and took a job driving a truck for Crown Electric Company. He delivered supplies to all parts of Memphis, but his favorite part of town was still Beale Street. It was there that he discovered a small recording studio known as Sun Records.

Sam Phillips owned the studio. Although Phillips was white, he had opened Sun Records mainly to give black musicians a chance to record their music. He loved the sounds of Beale Street and wanted to help bring the blues to radio listeners and record buyers.

But a person didn't have to be black to record at Sun—all kinds of musicians were welcome, as long as they could pay the three-dollar fee for cutting a record.

It was late summer of 1953 when Elvis Presley first walked into the studio at Sun Records. The woman who ran the office asked how she could help him.

"I want to make a record," Elvis replied.

"What do you sing?" she asked.

Elvis hesitated for a minute. He had listened to radio and records and live performances all his life—gospel, blues, country, pop, even opera. There weren't many kinds of music he didn't know or like.

"I sing all kinds," he replied.

"Who do you sound like?"

This time Elvis didn't hesitate. "I don't sound like nobody."

Elvis paid his fee and recorded two songs—"My Happiness"

and "That's When Your Heartache Begins." (Those recordings were lost before Elvis became a star.) Before he left, he asked the woman to keep him in mind if she came across anyone looking for a singer. She promised that she would.

What she didn't tell Elvis was that she had made a copy of his record. She thought Sam Phillips might be interested in hearing it.

Phillips had been struggling with a dilemma ever since he set up his business on Beale Street. He knew that there were a lot of white people who liked black music, but in the segregated South of the 1950s, many were embarrassed to buy it.

"I got to thinking how many records you could sell if you could find white performers who could play and sing in the same exciting, alive way as black performers," Phillips said. "I knew that if I could just find a white man with the sound and feel of a black man, I could make a billion dollars."

Phillips had friends—Scotty Moore and Bill Black—who played in a band. In July 1954 he had an idea. "I want you to meet a singer who was here at Sun a few months ago," he told them. "He's nineteen years old. His name is Elvis Presley."

Elvis and the two musicians spent hours in the studio experimenting with a blues song called "That's All Right, Mama." They recorded it, and on the flip side of the record they sang an upbeat version of the old bluegrass song "Blue Moon of Kentucky."

Sam Phillips distributed the record to local radio stations. No one was prepared for what happened next.

Popular disc jockey Dewey Phillips (no relation to Sam) of WHBQ, a radio station in Memphis, played both songs on his show. The phone lines lit up and telegrams began flooding the station. Listeners didn't know what kind of music they had just heard, but they knew they liked it.

Phillips played the songs over and over again—first "That's All Right, Mama," then "Blue Moon of Kentucky."

And he telephoned the Presleys.

"Mrs. Presley, I need to speak to Elvis," he said when Gladys answered.

"He's not here," she told him. "He went to the movies."

"Then go get him, please. I need to interview him on my show!"

That's how it all started. Elvis, Scotty, and Bill began traveling around the South, performing at schools and county fairs and shopping centers. At first they toured only on weekends. None of them could afford to quit their real jobs.

But they soon became so popular that they were able to work full-time on their music. They recorded more songs for Sam Phillips.

And Elvis's sound came to have a name. At first, it was called "rockabilly"—named for its combination of hillbilly country music and rhythm and blues. Soon the name changed to something else—rock and roll.

Elvis Presley, an untrained singer who could not read a note of music, was about to change the world forever.

From the time he was a young child, Elvis had studied the way gospel singers performed. They didn't sing just with their mouths. They put their whole bodies into their emotion-filled shows. Elvis decided to do the same with his songs.

He swiveled his hips. He shook his legs. He curled his lips and threw back his head when he sang.

One observer described an early performance this way: "Elvis had on a black coat and a pink shirt and pink socks and a sneer on his face. He stood behind the microphone five minutes before he made a move. Then he began to gyrate. The crowd went wild."

Many adults hated the way Elvis performed. They called him disgusting. They called him vulgar. They called him obscene.

But teenage girls loved Elvis Presley. They screamed and swooned and fainted when he sang. They broke through security blockades just to try to touch him. They bought hats and blouses and poodle skirts that said ELVIS. They collected Elvis posters, bubblegum cards, and ballpoint pens. They bought his records and played them over and over and over again.

Teenagers finally had their own hero and their own kind of music. And many of them didn't care at all whether their parents liked it or not.

Elvis soon came to the attention of music promoter "Colonel" Tom Parker, who persuaded the Presleys to hire him as Elvis's manager. In November 1955, Parker made a deal for RCA Records to buy Elvis's contract from Sun Records. The purchase price was $35,000—more than had ever been paid for a recording contract.

Elvis quickly recorded several smash hits for RCA—"Heartbreak

Hotel," "Don't Be Cruel," "(You Ain't Nothin' but a) Hound Dog," "Love Me Tender," "All Shook Up," and "Jailhouse Rock."

By late 1956, RCA was selling more than $75,000 worth of Elvis Presley records every day!

Elvis kept the promise he had made to his parents so many years before. He bought them each a pink Cadillac (even though his mother couldn't drive). And he purchased a twenty-three-room mansion, named "Graceland," in Memphis and insisted that his parents and his grandmother live there with him.

He made numerous television appearances, guest starring on programs hosted by Tommy and Jimmy Dorsey, Milton Berle, and Steve Allen.

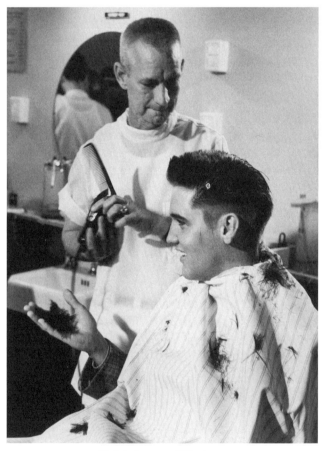

Elvis's famous GI haircut
(Copyright Elvis Presley Enterprises, Inc.)

Elvis's 1957 appearance on "The Ed Sullivan Show" drew higher ratings than any other show in television history, even though Sullivan insisted that Elvis be filmed above the waist when he sang, so the TV audience wouldn't be offended when Elvis wiggled his hips.

Colonel Parker made a deal for Elvis to star in a series of Hollywood movies. The first—*Love Me Tender*—was a major hit at the box office and was followed by *Loving You*, *King Creole*, and *Jailhouse Rock*.

In 1958 Elvis was drafted into the U.S. Army. More than fifty reporters and photographers recorded the shearing of his long locks into a GI hairstyle, making it the most photographed haircut in history.

Just a few weeks after he reported for basic training in Texas, Elvis received word that his mother was gravely ill. He returned to Memphis barely in time for a tearful farewell.

Heartbroken over Gladys's death, Elvis sobbed, "I'd give up every dime I own and go back to digging ditches, just to have Mama back."

He returned to military duty and was assigned to a base in Germany. That's where he met Priscilla Beaulieu, the fourteen-year-old daughter of an American officer stationed there. Elvis and Priscilla developed a deep friendship despite their difference in age. When Elvis's duty in Germany ended in 1960, he promised that he would do his best to bring Priscilla to the United States.

Priscilla moved to Memphis in 1962. Her romance with Elvis flourished, and they were married in 1967. Lisa Marie Presley, their only child, was born the following year.

Elvis had worried that his fans might forget him during the two years he spent in the Army. Colonel Parker was not going to allow that to happen.

He had been busy keeping Elvis's name and his records available to his millions of fans. When Elvis returned to civilian life, Parker signed him to another movie deal. Between 1960 and 1967, Elvis starred in twenty movies. But he was not happy.

Elvis wanted to be a singer, not a movie star. He worried that the popularity of rock and roll groups like The Beatles and The Rolling Stones meant that fans were no longer interested in his kind of music.

He was wrong.

Elvis in the 1970s (Copyright Elvis Presley Enterprises, Inc.)

He starred in a 1968 television special that was a huge success. He played to sold-out audiences in Las Vegas. He toured throughout the country. He even visited President Richard Nixon at the White House.

The Elvis of the late 1960s and early 1970s looked different than the Elvis of the 1950s. He was older and more mature. His hair and sideburns were longer than ever, and the grease and ducktail were gone.

He dressed different, too. Bell-bottom jumpsuits decorated with rhinestones and sequins took the place of pink-and-black outfits. Elvis sometimes wore his karate uniform when he sang. He sported heavy gold necklaces and bracelets and wore rings on every finger.

The fans loved him just as much as ever.

His songs "In the Ghetto," "Suspicious Minds," "Kentucky Rain," and "Burning Love" became mega hits. The 1973 satellite-TV special "Aloha from Hawaii" was broadcast to dozens of countries around the world and viewed by an estimated billion people!

But the happy times were soon to end.

In 1973 Elvis and Priscilla divorced. Elvis began overeating—fried peanut-butter-and-banana sandwiches were his favorite, followed by huge servings of ice cream. He soon became horribly overweight.

Elvis had been using prescription medications for several years for a variety of ailments. Now he began abusing those drugs. And he became increasingly dependent on alcohol.

Nothing could make him happy. He missed his mother. He missed Priscilla and Lisa Marie. He missed the good times he had had as a young man.

In July 1977 Elvis performed what was to be his last concert. Three weeks later—on August 16—he was found dead in his bathroom at Graceland. The coroner's report listed the cause of death as heart failure. He was forty-two years old.

Millions of Elvis fans reacted with grief and horror. Within hours after his death was announced, stores all over the world sold out of Elvis records and souvenirs. Tens of thousands of people descended on Memphis for his funeral.

Elvis was buried next to his mother at Forest Hills Cemetery, but it soon became obvious that the graves would have to be moved to protect the dignity of others buried in that cemetery. Only a few weeks after his death, the remains of Elvis and Gladys were moved to a garden behind Graceland. Vernon, who died in 1979, is buried there, too.

In a career that spanned more than two decades, Elvis Presley made thirty-three movies and 150 recordings. He sold over a billion records, more than any individual or group ever in the history of recorded music.

Graceland was opened to the public in 1982. Every year, tens of thousands of Elvis fans visit his home. They gaze in awe at the unique furnishings, the collection of cars and motorcycles, and the Hall of Records where Elvis's costumes and gold and platinum records are on display.

They visit gift shops near Graceland and buy T-shirts, posters, Elvis dolls, coffee mugs, and hundreds of other souvenirs. They buy tapes and CDs of his music. And they vow to never, ever forget him.

Why? Because Elvis Presley was the King—The King of Rock and Roll.

BIBLIOGRAPHY

Carter, Ian, Digby Fairweather, and Brian Priestly. *Jazz—The Rough Guide*. London: Rough Guides, 1995.

Daniel, Pete. *Lost Revolutions: The South in the Fifties*. Chapel Hill: University of North Carolina Press, 2000.

Guralnick, Peter. *Careless Love: The Unmaking of Elvis Presley*. New York: Little, Brown, and Company, 1999.

Guralnick, Peter. *Last Train to Memphis: The Rise of Elvis Presley*. New York: Little, Brown, and Company, 1994.

Halberstam, David. *The Fifties*. New York: Villard Books, 1993.

Marcus, Greil. *Mystery Train: Images of America in Rock 'n' Roll*. New York: Penguin Books, 1990.

Marsh, Dave. *Elvis*. New York: Times Books, 1982.

Williams, Martin T. *Smithsonian Collection of Classic Jazz*. Washington, D.C.: New York: Smithsonian Collection of Recordings. CBS Records, 1987.

Chapter Eighteen

DID YOU KNOW?
Tidbits of Tennessee Trivia

Geographically Speaking. . . .

Tennessee touches eight other states—Kentucky, Virginia, North Carolina, Georgia, Alabama, Mississippi, Arkansas, and Missouri.

The distance north to south in Tennessee is only about 100 miles, but the state stretches nearly 500 miles east to west. Tennessee encompasses 42,000 square miles within its borders. It is thirty-sixth in physical size of the fifty states.

More than 5,000,000 people live in Tennessee, making it seventeenth in population of the fifty states. Shelby County is Tennessee's largest county in number of residents; Pickett County is the smallest.

Murfreesboro is the town most exactly in the center of Tennessee.

Tennessee has thirty rivers within its borders. The three largest rivers are the Mississippi, the Cumberland, and the Tennessee.

The highest point in Tennessee is Clingman's Dome in the Great Smoky Mountains (6,643 feet above sea level). The lowest point is a spot along the Mississippi River near Memphis (182 feet above sea level).

Tennessee boasts the highest waterfall east of the Mississippi River—Fall Creek Falls, which is 256 feet high. Ruby Falls is the deepest cavern in the United States (1,120 feet below ground surface) and has the highest underground waterfall (145 feet).

Cumberland Caverns has the largest cave room in the eastern part of the United States, and the world's largest underground lake is the Lost Sea in Sweetwater.

The average winter temperature in Tennessee is forty degrees.

The average summer temperature is seventy-eight degrees. Tennessee's average annual precipitation is fifty inches.

A Capital Idea!
Rocky Mount was the capital city when Tennessee was still a territory. The capitol building there, built in 1770 of rough-hewn logs, is the oldest territorial capitol in the United States still standing on its original site.

Other cities and towns that have served as Tennessee's capital include Knoxville (1796-1812, 1817), Murfreesboro (1818-1826), and Kingston, which was capital for one day in 1807 (That was done to fulfill a treaty obligation made with the Cherokee Indians).

Nashville served as capital from 1812 through 1816. In 1826 it became the capital city again and was designated the permanent seat of Tennessee government in 1843.

The Tennessee State Capitol building was completed in 1859 and is one of the oldest working capitols in the nation. Its architect, William Strickland of Philadelphia, died before construction was finished. He is buried in a wall in the north portico of the building.

Who's in Charge Here?
William Blount served as the first and only governor of the territory of Tennessee. As of the year 2002, forty-eight men (and no women) have served as state governor. Two of them (Robert and Alf Taylor) were brothers. One (Austin Peay) died in office, and another (Ray Blanton) was removed from office three days before his term ended. Only one woman (Kate Bradford Stockton) has ever run for governor.

You Can "County" on This
Tennessee has ninety-five counties. Most are named for soldiers or statesmen. Some are named for geographical features. Two are named for Indians. Only one (Grainger County) is named for a woman.

What's for Dessert?
Several Tennessee companies help satisfy the nation's sweet tooth. In addition to Goo Goo Clusters, other sweet treats made in

Tennessee include King Leo peppermint sticks, MoonPies, Little Debbie Snack Cakes, Brock Candies, M&Ms, Blow Pops, and Mayfield Ice Cream.

Speaking of Slogans, Mottos, Nicknames, and Symbols. . . .

The official state slogan of Tennessee is "Tennessee—America at Its Best."

The state motto is "Agriculture and Commerce," taken from the wording on the state seal.

The most popular nickname for Tennessee is "The Volunteer State," so named because of the tremendous number of Tennesseans who volunteered to fight in the War of 1812 and the Mexican War. Tennesseans have continued to volunteer for military service at an enthusiastic rate for every war in which the United States has been involved.

Tennessee has 170 different species of flowers. The official wildflower is the passionflower. The official cultivated flower is the iris. More than 150 different kinds of trees grow in Tennessee. The state tree is the tulip poplar; the bicentennial tree is the yellowwood.

Tennessee's official animals include a state bird (mockingbird), game bird (bobwhite quail), sport fish (largemouth bass), commercial fish (channel catfish), wild animal (raccoon), insect (ladybug and firefly), agricultural insect (honeybee), butterfly (zebra swallowtail), amphibian (Tennessee cave salamander), and reptile (Eastern box turtle).

Let's not forget the state rocks and gems—limestone, agate, and Tennessee river pearls.

Last but not least are the state songs, and there are plenty of them: "My Homeland, Tennessee," "When It's Iris Time in Tennessee," "My Tennessee," "The Tennessee Waltz," "Tennessee," "The Pride of Tennessee," and, of course, "Rocky Top."

And Did You Also Know. . . ?

When white men first arrived, four Indian tribes—the Cherokees, Creeks, Chickasaws, and Shawnees—were living in the area that would become Tennessee.

Tennessee gets its name from *Tanasi*, the capital of the Cherokee Nation from 1721 until 1730.

Tennessee officially became a state on June 1, 1796, making it the sixteenth state to join the Union. The centennial celebration that should have taken place in 1896 wasn't held until 1897. Tennessee's bicentennial celebration was held on time in 1996.

In addition to Tennessee's three United States Presidents (Andrew Jackson, James K. Polk, and Andrew Johnson), two Tennesseans have served as Vice President (Andrew Johnson and Albert Gore, Jr.).

Tennessee has seven public universities—Austin Peay State University, East Tennessee State University, Middle Tennessee State University, Tennessee State University, Tennessee Technological University, University of Memphis, and University of Tennessee (with campuses at Chattanooga, Knoxville Martin, and Memphis).

BIBLIOGRAPHY

Beck, Ken. *Terrific Tennessee: The Best from the Volunteer State.* Nashville: Premium Press America, 1999.

Couch, Ernie and Jill Couch. *Tennessee Trivia.* Nashville: Rutledge Hill Press, 1991.

Lacey, T. Jensen. *Amazing Tennessee: Fascinating Facts, Entertaining Tales, Bizarre Happenings, and Historical Oddities from the Volunteer State.* Nashville: Rutledge Hill Press, 2000.

Tennessee Blue Book Online: 1999-2000 Millennium Edition. <http://www.state.tn.us/sos/bluebook/1999-2000/bbonline.htm> (July 17, 2002).